After completing his Senior Cambridge examination from St Xavier's School, Hazaribagh, **Malay Kumar Roy** did his graduation from St Xavier's College, Calcutta and Master's in English literature from Jadavpur University. Later, he spent nearly fifty years in the corporate sector where he worked in communications, which left little time for much else. After retirement, he writes about his memories of Hazaribagh where he spent his boyhood years.

An Elsewhere Place

Boyhood Days in Hazaribagh

Malay Kumar Roy

SPEAKING TIGER

SPEAKING TIGER PUBLISHING PVT. LTD
4381/4, Ansari Road, Daryaganj
New Delhi 110002

First published by Speaking Tiger in paperback 2017

ISBN: 978-93-86582-73-7
eISBN: 978-93-86582-74-4

10 9 8 7 6 5 4 3 2 1

Typeset in Arno Pro by SÜRYA, New Delhi
Printed at Thomson Press India Ltd.

For
Aloke Roy Chowdhury,
Aditi Nath Sarkar
and
Pritam Das

CONTENTS

How the Land Lay

In the years I lived there as a boy from the 1950s to the early '60s, Hazaribagh on the Chhotanagpur plateau was a magical place. Magical to me and to so many others who spent their school years there in those times. What this little collection attempts is to relive a boy's memories of its landscape, of the rhythm of seasons, of the changing colours of the earth, of its wildlife, of the joys and sorrows of village folk who were as elemental as the landscape they were part of, the interaction between visiting city folk and us who lived in Hazaribagh. And of the mood of the town, sitting tranquilly amid hills and forests.

Hazaribagh of that time was unhurried, and much of its landscape was close to town limits. Spacious homes on extensive grounds were set away from one another along lonesome roads and stood peaceably among fields and woodland. Deep forests of sal and shegun, banyan and eucalyptus, rolling hills, streams and meadows. Cultivated greenery and sisal plantations with their distinctive blue tone. Wildlife encounters. And the stillness of the landscape. Hazaribagh was all about atmosphere, a mood that stayed with you but challenged precise definition. Jojo Karlekar, a very old friend with whom I grew up, put it as well as anyone could: 'Hazaribagh,' he said, 'touches a boy forever.'

Our house was on the edge of town. It was a sprawling

bungalow with a large garden, side lawns, groves of mango, guava, custard apple and banana, rows of eucalyptus and a good-size vegetable patch at the back. The setting was spectacular. It faced the Patna–Ranchi highway. Across it, fields of sisal ended at the waters of Hazaribagh Lake. The rear of the house looked out on undulating fields, gullies, little streams and mustard fields which shone like sheets of gold in the winter sun. Living where I did, it was impossible not to be stirred by the immensity of the landscape, of sky to endless sky and turning seasons.

After all these years, the images are still vivid. Of biting sharp winter mornings, the countryside silent and disembodied in mist, frost on grass, waning afternoons, slow dusk and darkness falling. Villagers going home from the town, their creaking carts the only sound apart from the calls of grouse, partridge and foxes as they settled in for another cold night. Of bracing spring days with the hint of warmer days ahead, new leaves and buds everywhere, the trees a splash of colour. Of hot summer days, day-long dust storms, the glare and glint of mica specks in the roadside dust, the fields dry from the sun, on the vast brown expanse sudden clusters of trees that seemed like chips of jade from a distance, and cool nights on the terrace. Of rushing nor'westers, the swift change from hard sunlight to swirling clouds and near darkness. Of torrential monsoons, sheets of driving rain from the running sky, their hammering almost a roar, and at other times rain like fine spray, everything blurred and distant. Of the fields turning green after summer's heat. Of mellow autumns before winter came.

The town mirrored the serenity of the surrounding countryside. Hazaribagh, in the state of Jharkhand, was once a cantonment town during British times. Many Englishmen fell in love with Hazaribagh and other places in Chhotanagpur and built homes there. I still remember some lovely old houses, echoes from the past—Hampton Court, Balmoral, Saupins, Morris, Bee Hive (later acquired by St Xavier's School). And some others—Rosalynd, Kona Kuthi, Purbachal, Hill View, Leoden, Eucalypta, Gibraltar. These gave Hazaribagh an ambience all its own.

By the late '40s most Englishmen had left Hazaribagh but it still bears traces of some of the earliest town planning by the British. The old part of the town, known as Boddam Bazar, is believed to have been named after the officer who laid out its plan. Another familiar landmark is the busy Pagmal road.

The town's unassuming tranquility made it easy to forget its engaging past. Hazaribagh's etymology is generally accepted as the combination of 'hazari' meaning thousand and 'bagh' meaning garden. Another explanation is that the town takes its name from the villages of Okni and Hazari, the two names combining to Okunhazri.

The lovely old houses of Hazaribagh and the town's sights and sounds made up the ambience. A short walk took you to the heart of town and the mind calls back the atmosphere. The hum of students at St Columba's College set up by the Dublin University, at St Xavier's School, at Mount Carmel School for girls; the shouts of boys at play; the sound of bat and ball on our school playgrounds; the excitement of our school's Saturday evening movies; the Damodar Valley Corporation's office with its bustle and the quiet residential complex for their officers; the rolling sound of hooves as cadets of the Police Training College practiced their riding; our favourite eateries—Coffee House (hot chocolate milk at 50p, dosa at 25p) and Standard Restaurant when we were able to splurge (chicken curry/paratha at Rs 3.50, seekh kababs at Rs 2), the prices as close to accurate as I can remember; the rumble of long distance buses (operated by Lal Motor and Pearl Motor) plying to and from Hazaribagh town; the man on a rickshaw announcing over his loudspeaker the forthcoming films in one of the two movie halls (Picture Palace and Anand Bhavan). And something that has stayed vivid over decades is the memory of the Quarter Guard at the Court House which was also the office of the Collectorate. This armed worthy was required to call out 'Who goes there?' as darkness fell, only it came out sounding 'Hukum Sadar!' to anyone approaching, particularly the passing cycle-rickshaws. The interchange between the call of the Quarter Guard and the cycle-rickshaw drivers was sheer comedy. To the stentorian shout 'Hukum Sadar' the cycle-rickshaw driver gave two or three short bleats of his rubber horn. The Guard then repeated the cry 'Hukum

Sadar' and the cycle-rickshaw driver, in perfect imitation of the age-old military practice, cheerily responded with 'Fra-a-y-y-and!'

But what are these stories worth to the reader? At the time of putting these together, I saw them for what they were—essentially stories about the serenity of Hazaribagh that I wished to share. It made sense, I felt, to talk about these as I remembered them, of a time that was once, never to return.

Looking back, I found that some of the stories came across—by no means intentionally—as echoes of the contemporary engagement with specific things: the individuality of the girl child and the village boy, the implications of an inclusive education, and the value of preserving the natural landscape. Perhaps there could be relevance of a sort after all.

In some of the stories the names have been changed to protect privacy. Also the stories go back several decades. If I have erred in some details (names, places, etc.) due to a lapse in memory, this will have been beyond my control.

LOCAL COLOURS

Flowers for Cheli

A man stopped his bullock-cart alongside our front gate and came inside. He was middle-aged; his face darkened and lined by the sun. Clinging to his arm was his daughter, a girl of about fifteen, and that was how we met Cheli that warm spring morning.

The man said his name was Nanku Mahato and he was on his way to the town market with his nephew and his daughter, who had come along for the ride. He asked if he could draw water from our well. Such requests were common. Country folk from villages nearby on their way to the market with their produce—vegetables, fruits, grains—when thirsty, often stopped by our house for water.

When Cheli first came to our house with her father, I noticed was she was impossibly shy. A thin, wheat-complexioned girl with large, staring eyes, she was diffident about everything around her. She was particularly terrified of our gardener, who was really a harmless old man—I suspect it was his intimidating look that frightened her. But she took to my mother at once.

Soon, Cheli's visits began to take on a pattern. Twice or thrice a week, Nanku Mahato dropped her off on his way to the market. Cheli then spent the day at our house and returned in the evening with her father. Occasionally, when her father was late and it had grown dark, he unhitched his oxen under the gigantic mango tree beyond our gate, and settled down for the night. From our porch I could see the three of them—Nanku, Cheli and the nephew—as they went about preparing their evening meal. Cheli helped her father with the cooking, and in the light of the fire, I could sometimes see their faces in silhouette and shadow.

Though Cheli spent time with us, she was as shy as ever, and getting her to speak was difficult. When she did speak, it was in a low and curiously musical lilt; and it was only with Mother, whom she followed everywhere around the house like her shadow. She spent hours talking to her in that sweet low-pitched voice, and would eat only when Mother did. She divided her time between Mother in the kitchen and the courtyard and our garden outside.

In Hazaribagh of that time, we saw the vast landscape, trees, flowers and forest as a natural part of our lives, but Cheli seemed to find wonderment at the smallest things—a mauve wildflower, a sapling, a tendril curling up from some corner. She gazed at them, sometimes running her fingers lightly over the delicate leaves and petals. I could see why. Cheli's home was surrounded by their few acres, but her home did not really have a garden in the true sense.

At one end of our house, a frangipani tree was a splash of colour, lovely red flowers shrouding the branches and Cheli was enchanted with it. She was sure to stand under the branches and gather the flowers that had fallen on the ground. Mother had our gardener take a cutting, which she gave Cheli to plant at her home.

I think it was well over a year later when Cheli, on one of her visits, gave my mother a reed basket brimful with frangipani. Shyly, she informed her that it was from the tree that grew out of the cutting Mother had given her. Mother was so touched, she gave Cheli a long hug. She then made a pair of bangles out of the flowers and slipped them over Cheli's thin wrists. It was a wonderfully tender gesture and Cheli squealed with delight. Time and again she held up her hands, looking with joy at the delicate red petals against her skin.

Gradually, as Cheli grew older her visits were no longer frequent since, as her father explained, she was needed for the housework. And whenever she visited, I noticed a subtle change that had come over her. She was graver, quieter, even with Mother. Her concerns now were different, and more important—her father's crops, the sagging fence that needed fixing, her mother's fragile health, the bats that raided their guava tree at night, their two goats which were full of mischief and strayed if she was not careful.

One winter morning—it was a little more than three years since Cheli first came to us—Nanku Mahato came to share the news that Cheli's marriage had been arranged. The groom lived with his family about thirty miles or so from Nanku's village. The wedding was two weeks away, and Nanku insisted that we come.

Two days before the wedding, Mother came down

with a sudden high fever, and was terribly upset at missing the ceremony. Father had to stay back to look after her. In the early evening, our gardener and I went to the wedding in the village about two miles away, carrying our gift—a beautiful, finely wrought silver chain and a pair of matching bangles.

Seeing Cheli in her wedding dress, it was almost impossible to recall the skinny little girl whom we first saw years ago. She was now a self-possessed young woman, and she carried herself with poise. It was when she saw the gift that she was a child once more, joyfully showing her gift to others, much to my embarrassment. But when she saw that Mother wasn't with us, the hurt in her eyes was plain to see.

Returning home, I was made to answer question after question Mother asked me: did Cheli look pretty? What was she wearing? Did she miss her? How did the groom look?

A few days after the wedding, Nanku Mahato called on my parents. Cheli was now in her husband's home, and beamingly he told us that her in-laws were pampering her much more than they should. Cheli's initial interaction with her husband and his family though was far from happy. The day after the wedding, Cheli had set out for her new home. Well into the journey, Cheli discovered that in the hurry she had left one of her favourite things at home, and she pleaded that they turn back to pick it up. Her husband and his parents, irritated at her unreasonable behaviour, told her she could retrieve it when she visited next. They remonstrated. They coaxed. They made their displeasure clear, but Cheli was inconsolable and they had no option but to turn back and resume their journey the next morning.

When they reached home and saw what it was she had come back for, they went from bemusement to incredulity. Cheli had come back for her pair of flower-bangles, long since withered and crumpled, but once fresh and beautiful when Mother had put them lovingly on her wrists, and which she had treasured since that day more than three years ago.

Bhaglu's Passion

The boy raking the dry leaves at our neighbour's porch looked to be my age. Our neighbours were an elderly widow and her daughter—her other children having already settled in the metros. Her youngest daughter Rani, who lived with her, was in her early twenties and taught at a school. Mother and daughter lived quietly in their home, which was a fair distance from ours. This was where Bhaglu came every day, clearing away leaves and twigs, tending the garden and sometimes doing odd jobs around the house.

Bhaglu did his work with a kind of plodding deliberation. When clearing leaves, he methodically collected them in small piles. When putting away his rake, he walked slowly to the wall, carefully leaning the rake against it. When sweeping the courtyard, he did it slowly as if there was all the time in the world. He was nearly always slow in his reaction, and had a habit of repeating a request to make sure he had understood it. If Rani's mother said, 'Bhaglu, close the door, please', he would ponder gravely and then say to himself, 'Close the door', before doing it.

Bhaglu adored Rani, eagerly doing her bidding, and his joy was unmistakable when she praised him, which was often, for her affection for him was genuine. She was the protective mother hen and pampered him endlessly. Even when she rebuked him for doing something wrong, he earned no more than a mock-angry look.

Bhaglu could not read or write, and Rani tried patiently to teach him figures and alphabets, but to no avail. It took no special eye to see that this was not where Bhaglu's instincts lay. Apart from Rani, he kept to himself. He was by no means impaired, but his slowness gave most people the wrong idea, and this made Rani very angry. Whenever I visited Rani and her mother, I saw Bhaglu around the house, going about his chores in his slow, measured way. But there was something that was curious. Frequently, and nearly always in the late afternoons, when Bhaglu had finished his tasks, he would ask Rani if he could go to her little library. This was actually her cosy sitting room at one end of the house, doubling as her library, which ran along the length of two walls. She had a wide selection from literature, history and philosophy, and I loved borrowing from it. At one corner of the room was her gramophone—of the old, hand-cranking variety—and her records on 78 rpm were Western and Indian classical, and songs of Tagore.

Why Bhaglu wanted to spend time in Rani's library was beyond me. Whenever I asked Rani, she was invariably evasive, and hinted that I didn't really care to know. One evening, I made an unexpected visit to Rani's library. What I saw was astonishing. Rani was sitting by her gramophone, and music was playing. Bhaglu sat across her on the floor at the far corner of the room. Cross legged and upright, he sat with his eyes closed, moving his head imperceptibly to the music, and lost to everything else. It was a Western classical symphony, strangely haunting and sad, and I had not heard anything like this before. Like most boys my age, I had no exposure to classical music; our world was pop and rock 'n' roll, Cliff Richard and Elvis Presley. I tiptoed away, not wanting to break the moment.

Next day, I made a point of asking Rani. She said that the piece she was playing was one that Bhaglu insisted on listening to whenever he could. She couldn't explain this any other way except that inexplicably, it always moved him. She said it was a Rachmaninov symphony, and she had no clue why or how this particular composition touched him as mysteriously as it did. Certainly, Bhaglu himself could not say. Bhaglu showed no apparent ear for music but loved only this particular piece.

To say I was humbled isn't saying nearly enough. That night I asked my father, hoping he could perhaps come out with something that made sense. He confessed he was puzzled. Tentatively, this is what he said. Could it be that unlike many other art forms—poetry, prose and drama for example—music did not call for a background in education, nor an intellectual calibre? Could this be explained by a person's innate and atavistic connection to sound and harmony? I could not guess, but I have never forgotten the image of Bhaglu as he sat entranced by the strains of Rachmaninov.

An Escape for Birju

The first drops of rain fell when we were about six miles away from town on a biking trip along the Hazaribagh station road. Looking for shelter, we took the dirt track that branched off from the road and there, at three hundred yards or so, stood a hut. Grateful for the shelter, we wheeled in our bikes, the rain now a drenching downpour.

This was late August, the morning gloriously sunny when we set out, but we should have remembered that this was an uncertain time, somewhere between monsoon and autumn but not quite either.

The man who opened the door was not yet in his middle age. He was short, stocky, humour playing around his mouth and he looked quite amused to see my friend and me running breathless to come in out of the rain. He said he was Birju and he had a host's warmth as he cheerfully welcomed us in. He lived with his twelve-year-old son, and by profession he was a bird trapper like his father before him. We rarely saw men of his calling and Birju told us about the birds he trapped and sold for meat. Grouse and 'bageri', the local name for a bird as small as a sparrow, a top-of-the-table delicacy and pitifully defenceless. He said he made a tidy income from the birds he sold, and when we asked him if he was comfortable with his profession, he dismissed the idea with jolly unconcern. What could possibly be wrong in trapping birds? Did anyone ask a butcher, a poultry farmer or a fisherman how they felt about what they did for a living?

What I remembered most about Birju's hut was its little garden; nothing showy, just a modest patch of grass alive with the colours of periwinkle and hibiscus. At the back was a small clearing on which some maize grew. The place was peaceful, and Birju obviously knew his gardening. The rain had stopped, and the road and the jungle on either side were washed clean after the shower as we pedalled homeward. The station road was one which we did not usually take for our excursions, and after some months the morning with Birju had turned into a casual memory. Then one day in the beginning of summer, we decided to cycle again to Birju's dwelling. The dirt track was there, same as before, but the cottage was deserted. Part of the roof had collapsed, the windows were gaping sockets and the little garden was weeded over. The whole place had the look of decay.

One day, quite by chance, I met Birju in the town market. He said he had come to buy some gardening tools. I asked him why he didn't live in his hut anymore, and was surprised at what he said. One evening some months ago, he had got a very good price from an unexpectedly large catch. Two days later he dreamt that the birds were crowding him, and snapping at him vengefully. The problem was that this wasn't a one-off dream, but a recurrent one and it unnerved him. To compound the situation, his son caught a raging fever which wouldn't go away. So Birju went to the village ojha, a reed-thin medicine man. After hearing what Birju had to say, he sagely proceeded to unravel the mystery. The dream, he said, was all about the vengeful spirits of the dead birds and they were tormenting him through his son. Birju must atone through an elaborate ritual which the ojha would conduct; otherwise there would be no respite from his ordeal. Desperate with anxiety and fear, Birju went through with it, but it did him no good, his dreams and his son's illness were unrelenting.

This was the ojha's domain of arcane knowledge of the supernatural. Clearly, visiting fathers' sins on their children was a ploy to make Birju part with his money. All else having failed, Birju turned to the local dispensary, and slowly the medicines started to cure his son but he was still desperately weak. Whether it was the ojha's grim forecast or Birju's premonition I don't know, but Birju decided that he and his son were better off without his bird-trapper's profession. He had always liked gardening and was lucky when he got the job as chowkidar and gardener in a bungalow owned by a family which visited only once or twice a year. He was happy trimming the hedges and the lawn and tending to flowers and looking after the house. And the dreams of malevolent bird spirits and their accusatory beaks? They didn't come back.

Some who knew about this were cynical about the whole business and said that the events were unrelated and trying to connect them was silly romanticism.

Unrelated or not, the feeling wouldn't go away that all the strands—birds, bird-trapper, son, medicine-man—perhaps had converged somehow and Birju in his moment of epiphany may have reached his decision. And there was something else about Birju. His carefree jolliness had gone and his face now had the look of sober contentment.

Sarju's Bicycle

Sarju's father was a mechanic who repaired vehicles—buses, trucks and cars—passing through or starting from Hazaribagh town. Sarju, a skinny fifteen-year-old, sometimes helped his father. Not often though, because his father insisted he go to school, something that was denied to him in his own childhood.

A serious-looking boy, Sarju went to the local day school. He wasn't essentially bright in his studies but good enough to get through his exams. His real love—obsession, actually—was his bicycle. It was of venerable age, and it had been used by Sarju's father in his youth before he bequeathed it to his son. As far as I remember, it was an old Hercules model, long past its prime and could well be ready for the scrapyard. The one thing that kept it running, and running well, was Sarju's devotion to it and the elaborate care he took of it every day. You could see him tinkering with it after school—oiling the chain, fixing the pedal bars, tightening the brake shoes, cleaning the tyres and mudguard, polishing the entire body. All his efforts didn't of course make it gleam because nothing could revive it from its aged look, but they certainly kept it serviceable and good to go.

The medium of transport in Hazaribagh and its outlying villages was principally the bicycle; it was a necessity rather than a luxury. It was what carried students to class, office-goers to the workplace, milkmen on their deliveries and villagers to town and back home. Most of Sarju's schoolmates had their own cycles. This is where Sarju's problems began. Because he was poor, poorer certainly than the other boys, he was often looked down on by some of his classmates in attitudes ranging from mild to sneering contempt. His old bicycle only made matters worse. Its antiquity drew jeers and humiliating comparison with the others' shiny cycles. Sarju's chief tormentor was a rough-looking classmate of his who belonged to a privileged section. He was Jagdish. Hopelessly spoilt, he was something of a petty tyrant with his collection of hangers-on. It wasn't that Sarju did not show his unhappiness at the treatment he continuously received from Jagdish and company. His misery was apparent, but he bore the taunts silently and this only spurred the gang to unmerciful jeers. 'Sarju, did your bike belong to your grandfather?' 'Do something for us Sarju, get this junk out of our sight.' 'Sarju, is your cycle carrying you, or is the wind pushing you along?' 'Sarju has no shame. If his cycle doesn't embarrass him, nothing will!' These were some of the cruel swipes at which the young are somehow so casually adept. But one thing stayed unchanged, no insults could deviate Sarju's loving care for his bicycle.

One day a cycle race was set up by Sarju's school and boys from outside the school were also allowed to join in. There was much excitement and Sarju's father persuaded him to participate. For poor Sarju this was fresh misery because Jagdish and his friends made it a point to make him more miserable than he already was. The most unfeeling gibe came when Jagdish and his acolytes said it was beneath them to compete in an event which Sarju and his bicycle were a part of.

The race day was on a fine autumn morning. A large crowd had gathered, the speaker was calling out to the competitors to line up, supporters were cheering their favourites and many felt that outsiders notwithstanding, the first three prizes were sure to go to Jagdish and company. The cyclists lined up. Sarju was at the far end and as they were getting ready, a barrage of insults came his way. 'What are you doing here? Get out, get out at once,' said one of Jagdish's pals.

The race—five laps around the field—started and they were off. After three laps, Jagdish, two of his friends and two boys from outside the school pulled away from the rest. On the fourth lap, things started to change. The two outsiders were in the lead, Jagdish and company falling back. The last lap was on. The two who were not from the school but allowed to compete began to draw further and further away, while Jagdish and his friends continued to fall back. The race ended. The two outsider cyclists came in first and second and someone else from the school who was quite unfancied took the third position. And there was a twist to the whole show. Sarju came in fourth.

The prizes were given out and then something unexpected happened. The judge, a prominent-looking man in a cravat, decided to announce a special prize.

While examining the bicycles before the race, he was much impressed by a particular one. It was well past its best days but its condition was admirable. It showed, he said, how dedicated upkeep could give new life to a machine and keep it from going obsolete. The special prize, the judge said solemnly, was for something more than the race. It was about protecting what you had. Sarju was uncomprehending about it all, but the pride on his father's face was something to see.

Around a month later something else occurred. This was unrelated to the race but I thought it was in the nature of a neat postscript. It was a Sunday evening in early winter. The town was quiet and there was very little activity. Suddenly Jagdish's father was crying out in alarm. Without warning his wife had fallen gravely ill, her old asthma flaring up. The doctor was needed immediately but there was nobody around. Jagdish was sleeping and efforts to wake him up failed; in all likelihood his sleep-fuddled mind could not grasp the seriousness of the situation. It was some time before he realized the urgency and prepared to take off on his bicycle to fetch the doctor. The news of the illness had spread a good deal earlier. Sarju, as soon as he heard of it, had got on his trusty cycle, sped as fast as he could and had knocked on the doctor's door. A cycle rickshaw was called. The doctor got in and Sarju led the way, pedalling furiously. They reached the house well before Jagdish had even got to the doctor's home.

The timely treatment took care of the situation.

Jagdish's father was endlessly thankful to Sarju for having come to the rescue. He remembered him from the school race. In a show of his appreciation and generosity, he said he would buy him a new bicycle. He insisted, but Sarju said he was fond of his old bicycle and didn't want a new one. Not to be put off, Jagdish's father said he intended to speak to Sarju's father—he would like at least to pay Sarju's school fees for one whole term.

I don't know if this came about, but Sarju had won the race when it mattered.

Sukhni's Blessing

We saw the old woman when my father and I were nearly home after a walk on a cold winter morning. She was sitting under a tree by the roadside with a small pile of fresh vegetables—small, firm cauliflowers, plump tomatoes, white-purple turnips. She sat huddled in the cold, gaunt and withered. What was strange was that she had chosen this spot to do her selling, because for the village folk, the road was the way to town where they sold their goods. This simply wasn't the place where anybody would stop to buy.

From her fragmentary information, I was able to piece together the story of old Sukhni. She used to live with her son in a nearby village. She was a widow of some years and her son worked on their small patch of land, ploughing, planting and picking. He neither asked nor allowed his mother to work, except for the weeding she sometimes helped him with. Bhek Ram, she said, was a good and devoted son and she was blessed that he was beside her in her old age. Lately though, Bhek Ram was determined to leave the village and work in a town, so that he could earn more for the both of them. The thought frightened Sukhni. She pleaded that he stay back, saying that what his father had left her and what they earned from their farm was adequate to get by and that she was content. He had not listened to her, and had gone off to Giridih, a town about 70 miles away where he found work for what he said was good pay.

Old Sukhni doted on her son and missed him terribly—he had been away for two weeks. She was old and frail, far too old to carry her produce to the town market. She couldn't even carry it to the roadside without the help of a lad in her village. She was always weary and depressed from the futile wait for customers. But what actually hurt her the most was the absence of her son and her loneliness. Her only wish was to live her last days in the security of her son's presence. Sukhni said all this in a matter-of-fact, conversational way. Then she fell silent, eyes bleak with pain.

As soon we came home, Father sent our help to Sukhni to buy as many vegetables from her as he could. But he knew this was a partial solution at best. He stayed sombre all day long, something quite against his nature. That night, he told us that he was arranging to pick up vegetables from Sukhni every day, and he organized something more. He persuaded some people who lived in the town's power station close to our house to also buy vegetables from Sukhni daily, in rotation, in addition to what he himself purchased. The arrangement worked well. When I went to her place by the roadside one day, she wasn't there. I walked to her hut, and there she was, washing fresh radishes from her patch. She told me that her vegetables were selling out and she was able to get back before midday.

Father was troubled by her sadness and went to see her whenever he could. Old people and children, he used to say, needed equal measures of care. As unobtrusively as he could, he tried to figure out if there was anything she needed. Old Sukhni would not say, but father was able to gently prise out her immediate need: a new blanket to keep her warm in the cold nights.

Father took it to her the next day and I feared she would refuse outright. To my relief, she didn't and seemed touched by his concern. More followed—a pair of sandals as the old ones had worn out, a new kerosene lamp, a sackful of flour for which she couldn't travel to town, a scarecrow he arranged to be put up on her vegetable patch. Father spent time with her, chatting about her family, and about the days gone by. Once Sukhni caught a high fever and Father was not taking chances. He took the doctor to her, who gave her medicines for three to four days, until recovery. When we could, Father or I kept her company. Sukhni's son had been away for more than three weeks by now. He sent her a message that only said he was well. Father was undisguised in his anger towards Bhek Ram. He said often that Bhek Ram was an unfeeling and uncaring son of a loving mother. But I thought he was wrong; young Bhek Ram cared enough for his mother to take himself away from his roots for their sake. Father dismissed this as plain nonsense.

One day towards the month's end, we went to Sukhni's home. Evening was closing in, there was mist on the fields and hedges. A short distance away, we could see Sukhni's hut and the sudden spurt of a flame as she lit her oil lamp. She did not look distressed or careworn and said she had news to share. Bhek Ram had sent a message that town life—with its pace, confusion and bustle—was not for him, and that he could not take his employer's rudeness any longer. He missed his little farm and missed his mother more. He was coming home in a week.

Sukhni's relief was palpable and Father told her cheerfully that she had nothing more to worry about. We were sitting on her little porch floor and by way of celebration, she lit her chula, made thick, round chapatis and served them with pieces of gur. We ate in comfortable silence and Sukhni sat down beside Father. Then she did a strange thing. She stretched out her hand—her bangle hanging loosely on her bony wrist and in danger of falling away—and craning forward, ran her old fingers uncertainly along my father's face. Eyes closed, she murmured low and long. The moment froze in my memory—Father keeping stock-still and Sukhni with her low-pitched monologue. In the dim light of the lamp, I saw that her face was wet with tears. Startlingly, so was Father's—though I was certain he had absolutely no idea what she was saying. But I—my Hindi being better than Father's—understood. Sukhni was not giving Father the usual blessing of a long life. What she was praying for was that other people in her village, which was her world, would be fortunate enough to receive the same sympathy and concern that she had received. And she prayed that Father never lose the outreach of compassion with which he was blessed.

Abruptly, she composed herself, and went to make tea, which we drank from her shiny brass pots. Then she smiled, and her smile glowed brighter and warmer than her cooking fire.

It gladdened me that Father was wrong about Bhek Ram. He continued to be a dutiful and loving son, caring for his mother's every need till the day she died peacefully in her bed three years later.

Satlal and Uncle

'*Pet me bahut dard hai*,' said Satlal of his son Shamlal who was moaning in agony because of a stomach ache. This was the first and only time I remember seeing Satlal distraught and without his usual poise.

Satlal was the washerman who came to our house once a week to collect clothes for washing and ironing. His presence was distinctive, an air of gravity and reserve which was enhanced by the dress he always wore—long white shirt, knee-length white dhoti, white pagri, all starched and immaculate on his lean, dark frame. He hardly spoke other than when necessary and I was somewhat in awe of him. Satlal was fastidious. When he collected clothes for washing, he made a point of folding them as though they were freshly pressed. I had the temerity to ask him once why he did that. He gave me a frosty look and asked if I could tell him why not. That, of course, was that. His equanimity never failed him. The scene Father and I hugely enjoyed was when sometimes Mother, unhappy with the washing, complained. In such situations, Satlal listened in serious silence, shaking his head as if to say, 'I give up'. There was a hilarious situation one day; one of my school shirts had a torn collar. 'How could this happen?' Mother complained. Satlal gave this serious thought and his reply was disarmingly artless, '*Theek bataya apne maji, lekin mujhe sachi nahin maloom. Soch raha hoon yeh hua kaise*?' Father burst into uncontrollable laughter; Mother was piqued but couldn't help joining in.

So it was a surprise when Satlal came to my father, all off-balance, with the news of Shamlal's predicament. He pleaded we come at once and we set out for Satlal's home. Poor Shamlal was in bed, face contorted in pain, and his mother stood by, crying silently. The doctor could not be contacted as he had left town and it came down to my father to do something for his relief. Father was carrying his small medicine box with him, our home being a repository of all kinds of tablets and mixtures. Shamlal's symptoms were obvious—this was a case of acute gastritis. Father, armed with his own experience of similar afflictions in our family, gave him a pill and a tonic to lessen the pain. We waited, and after about half an hour he began to feel better and his face relaxed. Father asked Satlal to repeat the medicine in the evening and twice the next day. We were back at Satlal's the day after and saw the doctor examining Shamlal. His pain had returned, though not strongly, and the doctor concurred that this was gastritis brought about by reckless eating habits. He prescribed the same medication, adding one of his own.

For the next few days, Father visited Satlal's son every day, and when his recovery picked up, every other day or so. Satlal insisted on Father monitoring his son's recovery, and Father took this up in all seriousness—visiting, adjusting the medicines as instructed by the doctor, making certain that Shamlal's food was spice-free, and sometimes waiting in case there was any sudden recurrence of pain.

Things were going smoothly in the Satlal home. Shamlal's recovery was slow but consistent, and that was the best way, said the doctor. Unexpectedly, things took a bad turn one day. The pain returned; it was not as savage as the last time, but bad enough and so it was back to where it started. It was easy to find out why his pain had come back. Getting better by the day, Shamlal became careless and had gorged on the tart-sweet tamarinds from the tree close by—precisely the kind of thing he shouldn't have done. Father was angry but there was nothing else to do but start the treatment all over again. Over the next few days, his condition swung between recovery and relapse and Satlal and his wife were desperate with worry. For the first time Father seemed uncertain but persisted with the medication after consulting the doctor. Finally Shamlal began to get better, and though full recovery was still some time away, his illness was beginning to be seen as a thing of the past. The doctor suggested Shamlal could go back to school in about a week.

It was around then that Satlal brought another piece of news. His uncle Jugal chacha, who as I recall lived in Barhi, was coming to stay for a few weeks. Satlal looked happy but nervous; clearly he revered his uncle and was anxious to make a good impression. Jugal chacha was no ordinary man, he kept saying in a fever of nervousness and reverence. A few days later he came to us with his

Jugal chacha and we could see straightaway why Satlal was on edge. Short, plump and in his middle age, he came across as an affable man, but the obvious thing was that he affected a mellow tolerance of those around him, as though he was forever amused at their failings. He made no attempt to disguise the fact that he thought of himself on a higher plane of practical wisdom. Soon we were swamped by the weight of his knowledge—sometimes by way of advice, sometimes censure and sometimes authoritative guidance. Mali, our gardener, was his first victim. Jugal chacha gently admonished Mali—who was an experienced gardener—for the way he was pruning the hedges. It was all wrong, he said, and was bound to do more harm to the plants than good. He pointed out Mali's error in caring for the roots of the mango trees whose branches, when in bloom, needed the right kind of strength against strong summer storms. And, much to Mali's annoyance, he proceeded to demonstrate the right way of going about it. To the carpenter who came one day to fix my study table, Jugal chacha pointed out that whatever he did, the repair wasn't going to last, judging by the way he was stiffening the legs. The carpenter left in a huff and had to be coaxed back.

Mother was the third victim. With avuncular expansiveness, he explained that she must really be firm with our household helps, and supervise more strictly the upkeep of the house, otherwise it was bound to go to rack and ruin. Did she know, for example, that the front porch was not being swept properly? Or that the cobwebs in the outhouse had not been cleared since he last saw them? Tongue-in-cheek, Mother told us that it would have been no great loss if Jugal chacha hadn't visited us at all—we were not really worthy of his wisdom anyway. And she wondered if it ever struck him that the less we saw him, the more we liked him.

The best was reserved for Father. Since the time Jugal chacha came to stay with Satlal's family, he had persistently disapproved of Shamlal's treatment. With a sort of bored contempt, he watched as Father went about monitoring the medicine to make sure the doctor's advice was followed. '*Koi kaam ka nahin*,' he often told Satlal, to his deep embarrassment. All this fancy treatment was unnecessary because the remedy was quite simple. By now Satlal had lost much of his earlier enthusiasm about his chacha and was silently counting the days before he would return to Barhi. 'Another five days,' he told my father with weary resignation one day. The strain of chacha's constant counselling was taking its toll on him but much more on his wife who had to put up with him all day.

Father took the doctor along for a final check-up before Shamlal went back to school. By now he had recovered and barring restrictions on food, was almost as good as new. Satlal and his wife could not thank Father enough and would never forget his kindness, they said feelingly. At this point, Jugal chacha came in. With quiet authority he told everyone he had always suspected that Shamlal's treatment was flawed since nearly three weeks had passed and he had not recovered fully. Therefore he had prepared a 'totka', his own concoction, and had administered it. '*Maine khudh hi ek puria banake ladke ko de diya, aur dekhiye sirf ek dose me woh bilkul fit ho gaya. Abhi to woh khelega-kudhega,*' he announced with unblushing directness. The expression on Father's face was a study.

Samru

A little way from the town centre was a tea shop by the roadside. It hummed all day till closing time, and drew all kinds of customers—students, office workers, passing tourists, and also those of the less prepossessing variety. They thronged and jostled for the limited sitting space and for their hot tea, samosas, pakoras and sweets. It was a place where we went often.

The two boys—fifteen or, at the most, sixteen years old—serving the customers could not be more different from each other. One had the cheerfulness and cheekiness of his age, chatty as he served customers and standing by with the pleading expectation of a tip. As for the other, his expression belied his age. It was unvaryingly neutral, almost flat, neither friendly nor unfriendly. He showed no welcome, never got into conversation and served without a smile. If a customer berated him for being late, he made it a point to delay the service further. He was indifferent to tips, and no one crossed him. He was Samru, and he lodged in the house of a local trader for whom he did odd jobs in the evenings and on his day off from the shop.

I was enjoying my tea and samosas one day, when two young men came and sat at a table. Coarse and loutish, they were of a type one always found in any town. They talked loudly, made remarks about the passing girls and, true to their type, were spoiling for trouble. They then picked on Samru. They shouted at and cursed him for being late with their tea, but Samru did not respond except to say that their cups were on the way. This only inflamed them more and their abuses became violent. I still remember the only riposte Samru made during the whole unsavoury situation. To one of the bullies who shouted '*Chai kabhi banaye ho*?', Samru's reply was immediate: '*Chai kabhi piye ho*?' The two young men were shocked into pausing. No one dared to talk back to them as he did, and this could not be tolerated since they had a 'reputation' to protect. They left mouthing expletives, and threatened that the matter wasn't over.

What happened after some days was not something I saw, but heard from an acquaintance who was a regular at the shop. It went something like this:

Returning home in the afternoon, I came across a small crowd milling around someone lying on the ground. It was Samru. He had been savagely beaten, his body a mass of terrible bruises. One of his eyes was swollen shut from the beating, and there was more horror—multiple cigarette burns on his back and legs. Absolutely brutal. Samru had served me many times, and as I held him, I asked him again and again who was responsible. For some time there was no reply, then he started to cry. He did not cry as a boy does, but with the rasping, racking sobs of a man and it was clear to me that his humiliation was beyond the pain. Not knowing what to do, I listened helplessly.

Samru never spoke about it. He did not blame anyone,

but we were certain that the two louts had done this. The sad thing was that no one dared to intervene. The bullies had a notorious reputation and were given a wide berth. Samru went back to the tea shop after some days and acted as if nothing had happened. He brusquely dismissed any show of sympathy. The astonishing thing was that the bullies continued to visit the tea shop, and never let up on their taunting and throwing insults at Samru, who put up with it all without a word.

Weeks passed and the whole incident was remembered as a kind of aberration for Hazaribagh with its untroubled and uneventful lifestyle. Then one day there was further sensation. On their way back from the town's lonely outskirts, which was a favourite with walkers, some boys saw one of the town bullies. His cycle was on its side, and he was lying on the rock-strewn ground, almost unconscious with pain, his cheek split open, blood pooling. His friend was called and as they were carrying him back, they saw that the injury could not be explained by the fall alone. His back bore marks of repeated beating, and the finger of one hand had been deliberately broken.

Townsfolk spoke of the incident in whispers and no one could guess what may have happened. Samru was automatically ruled out, given his age and disposition. But the question remained—who could have planned this diabolical thing and carried it out? Most of us felt it had to be the work of a rival ruffian. The injured bully brushed it off as an accident which, of course, was understandable since his ego was at stake. I asked Samru often, but he gave no reply. Once when I persisted, he looked up and I froze. The look was feral and triumphant and at that moment I could not recognize the Samru we knew. Then the look passed. Most of us were convinced that an act such as this was beyond Samru to carry out alone, and so far as we could tell, he appeared to have no close friends. Perhaps he was gloating? Guessing what really happened on that lonesome road got us nowhere.

It was a few weeks before our hoodlum hero ventured again into the tea shop, friend in tow. Samru went up to serve them, no expression on his face whatsoever. But I sensed something curious, something totally unexpected. As Samru came up to take their order, they stiffened visibly, fear unmistakable on their faces. They finished their tea and left in a hurry.

Father and Mali

The conversations of my father with our gardener—Mali, as we called him—were an unending source of comedy. Mali, well past middle age and wizened by the sun, was a man wise to the world of trees, plants and flowers. He was a skilled gardener, besides being an overall handyman around the house. As a gardener, Mali liked to keep things simple, planting flowers according to the seasons, and it was especially from November to March that the garden came alive with its winter crowd of cosmos, marigold, dahlia, rose, flox and pink.

Father took a deep interest in the garden and earnestly shared his ideas with Mali. Father had some fixed notions. He had a horror of flower beds on the side lawns and wanted them to be free of everything but grass. Mali would point out that this was not the fine 'durba' grass but rough crab grass, typical for Hazaribagh. 'Nevermind, it's grass after all,' would be Father's reply. Another impasse was Mali pruning branches. 'Why doesn't he leave the branches alone? Why doesn't he let them spread naturally?' He complained often.

The platform for real mirth though was elsewhere. The truth was that Father's enthusiasm far outran his knowledge of things horticultural. What this did was create uproariously hilarious situations. We were accustomed to the format: Father's animated proposals, Mali's polite boredom, Father getting more and more exasperated that he wasn't getting through to Mali, and Mali declining to take him seriously. One day Father saw a row of gourd vines that Mali had planted in our vegetable garden. Struck by the sight of fragile white flowers, off he went in search of Mali with an original idea. Wouldn't it be great, he tried to persuade Mali, if the vines were planted in the front garden? The garden would come alive with countless small white flowers. Mali was speechless, but responded heroically. Very good idea, he said, but when the flowers turned to gourds, what then? 'Just pluck 'em,' was Father's unperturbed reply. Mali was looking beseechingly at Mother who was doing her best not to giggle.

Another day, on the field behind our house, Father saw a small mustard patch, bright in the sunlight. Father had an inspiration: why not have mustard patches in our front garden? He was sure they would light up the place. By now Mali's forbearance had begun to run out, and with complete seriousness he suggested that perhaps Father could also consider installing a crushing plant for mustard oil: '*Tel ka ghani baitha dijiye.*' Father was miffed but I often wondered if they actually enjoyed their exchanges.

On an afternoon in autumn, I found Father in the garden, almost inarticulate with exasperation, and his anger was real. Planting for winter, Mali—in total disregard for Father's fondness for clear green lawns—had dug up the garden to make flower beds. The entire garden from the entrance to the porch, and from side to side, taking in the two lawns, was one great scar. Heaps of dark brown earth were turned up, giving the entire ground the unsightly look of a construction site. Father's disappointment was such that he refused to sit out on the porch, and for days sat at the back in the shade of the mango grove, looking out to the fields and the distant rolling hills. He refused to speak to Mali, but Mali's composure was intact. He went about his work without a word of regret and if he was hurt by Father's temper, he did not show it. Slowly the scars faded. The lawns, the central flower bed, the rows past the drive up to the front of the house were filled with tender green seedlings. Over days they grew rapidly and father went back to his original sitting place by the front porch.

Curiously, Mali had planted seeds of chrysanthemum—no other flowers, and I couldn't get over the feeling that this winter our garden was going to look monotonous and featureless. Mother thought so too and, privately, we blamed Mali for what we were sure was going to be a dull garden whereas it could have been ablaze with the colour of winter flowers.

In the days that followed, the saplings grew tall and luxuriant, the countless buds now fuller and firmer. We didn't get the chance to ask Father what he thought, partly because he felt that this was one unsavoury episode he had no choice but to get through, and partly because he was busy preparing to leave for Calcutta on a long trip. Days passed, the bushes and the buds stayed as they were till one day the first blossoms appeared, as though tentative against the oncoming chill of winter. Then they came out in a rush, and soon our garden was covered with small, tender blossoms. They were all white and I remembered that Mali had gone all the way to Ranchi to make sure that all the seeds were only white chrysanthemum.

The flowers grew bigger and day long they were radiant in the sunlight. By the time the day of Father's return came around, the flowers were in full bloom—large, white as snow and beautifully formed. That night when Father was returning, Mother and I waited for him on the front steps. In the stillness of the night, we gazed at the garden spellbound. The moon was full and the surrounding countryside was silent. But the garden was a miracle. It was a sweeping wave of pristine white chrysanthemum which seemed to glow under the cold, hard light of the moon. Never had I seen a garden so luminous, so dream-like; it was almost otherworldly. Guiltily I recalled my earlier reservations, and I knew that no mix of colour could come close to the breathtaking sea of white that stretched before us. Crossing the gate, Father entered. For a while he did not speak, looking on quietly. He did not immediately go inside, preferring to sit out in the November cold.

In the morning he went up to Mali who was picking green peas for Mother's kitchen. I was wondering if Father felt diffident about his earlier show of temper. That wasn't quite so, but he was not his usual jovial self either. With grave courtesy, he apologized to Mali for having criticized him. He was wrong, of course, and he thanked Mali for giving an aging man a small gift of wonder that was the garden in the night time.

Father died two years later after a brief illness and we came to Calcutta where I began my graduate studies. A year or so later when I went back to Hazaribagh for a school reunion, the first thing I did was go to the house. Mali came running to greet me; he was still wiry and nimble but there was a tiredness about him that wasn't there before. The house stood silent and sad, but sadder still was the garden. Plants grew, the grass was trimmed but somehow it had the look of casual indifference, as though maintaining it was no more than an irksome task. I commented on it and Mali said that in Father's time gardening was fun and that he always enjoyed Father's interest, particularly his odd and whimsical ideas. '*Ab kiske liye karoon? Tum log to aate nahin ho; ghar to khali parah hai; ab aur mann nahin lagta mera.*' To that I had no answer.

Found and Lost

In the near complete darkness the only light was the glow of the cigarette as my father smoked and chatted on the front porch with my brother who was home on leave from Calcutta. It was typical August weather in Hazaribagh: overcast sky, showers from light to hard drizzle, the trees in brooding outline and the monotonous drip-drip of rain as it fell on leaves. The late evening quiet was abruptly broken. There were three of them, villagers returning home. Babbling in excitement and fear they said that a huge bear was lurking outside our gate. It must be shot before it killed somebody. This was a surprise. We had once come across a lone bear ambling along in the woods, but a bear sitting by our gate was never an experience.

My brother took the gun, but held it negligently, cynical about the villagers' story, and he was right. When we approached the bear, it shuffled and moved, except it wasn't a bear at all. It was a man well into middle age, tall, huddled under a thick blanket and totally wet from the rain. Our flooding relief came with the terrible thought of what might have happened if we had taken the villagers' word. They were treated to an angry mouthful from Father. He didn't spare the stranger either. What on earth did he mean, skulking outside the house in the rain? Why couldn't he come inside for shelter? The man took the berating without a word. He was brought to the house where he dried himself, was given dry clothes that belonged to Father, and was given a hot meal. Throughout he was silent, clutching his sad little bundle. Getting him to say anything looked impossible and finally he said his name was Bhiku—short for, as our Mali explained later, Bhikari.

In the morning I went with Father to make purchases for Bhiku: dhotis, a pair of shirts and canvas shoes. By the time we got back Bhiku had caught a chill and was running fever and so any conversation with him was out of the question. We put him in Mali's room and all that we wanted to know had to keep till he was better.

A day later there was a visit from another stranger. He was Bhiku's relative and had been looking for him for the past two days, till he was told of the night of the incident at our home. His village was four miles away and he had come to take Bhiku back. He would have to wait till Bhiku got better, we told him. The man, Nandu, was Bhiku's brother-in-law and they were from the same village. His sister and Bhiku were married for more than fifteen years. The couple were completely devoted to each other and were content with their little farm and simple needs. A year ago Bhiku's wife died after a sudden illness and that had left him a broken man. He sold his small patch of farmland and, at the insistence of Nandu and his wife, came to live with them. They cared for him as best they could. Bhiku had been a cheerful, outgoing man till he lost his wife. Of course he missed her terribly. Bhiku hadn't smiled since his wife died, Nandu said with a shake of his head. But where was Bhiku going the night we found him at our gate? We asked Nandu. He had no idea, but Bhiku sometimes wandered off and they had no end of trouble bringing him back. Nandu was wondering if Bhiku was losing his mind.

As it turned out Bhiku stayed with us for the whole week because the fever took a while to subside. He was as uncommunicative as ever but did as he was told and had his meals and medicines on time. He was a strange presence in the house, silent, not encouraging any conversation and replying only when we spoke to him. With gentle persistence my parents tried to get him to open up and had a small measure of success. Where was he headed that night? Somewhere... he couldn't recall. Could he try? Ranchi, was the monosyllabic reply. Why Ranchi? Did he know anyone there? No answer. My lasting memory of Bhiku was his silence, and the way he stared at the fields as he sometimes sat on the lawn. Even Mali couldn't get close to him. It wasn't that he was churlish, but as though he had lost all wish to have anything to do with people. The only sign of interest that I saw during the whole time was one morning when Bhiku sat under our neem tree. Two squirrels were frolicking and at play, darting here and there and for an instant this brought a shadow of a smile to his face.

The bundle that Bhiku constantly kept by his side was a mystery but I was told reproachfully, and in no uncertain terms, not to pry. It didn't matter in the end though, and it happened this way:

The day before Nandu came to take him back, Mother asked Bhiku if he would like to keep his things in a little suitcase she could spare. When Mother brought it to him, he made no attempt at privacy, emptying the bundle and putting his things one by one in the case. It was a strange assortment of odds and ends. A photograph of a young woman. The print was faded but clearly it was his wife in the early days of their marriage. A set of silver ankle payels. A kurta. An old wristwatch with Roman numerals. A metal torch. And most curious of all, a flat, small and empty wooden box without a lid.

Nandu came the next day and when we said goodbye to Bhiku he did something that was out of keeping with his attitude over his week with us. He turned to my parents and my brother and folding his hands he held them to his forehead and bent low, without speaking a word. It seemed to me that this simple gesture was much more than anything he might have said. I took Nandu aside and asked him what it was with the wooden box. It was where Bhiku's wife kept her pet squirrel at night, and after her death, Bhiku had released it in the fields. We watched the two of them leave, and soon they were out of view at a turn in the road. 'I hope he is all right,' Mother said wistfully.

Nandu kept his promise to let us know how Bhiku was doing, and dropped by about once a week on his way to town. Bhiku was well in their care, but was consumed by heartache. It was one of my first real experiences of what grief could do to a man.

Two months later Nandu came to us, distraught. Bhiku had disappeared again; four days and no sign of him. Nandu was frantic, his wife was in tears, and they were searching for him everywhere. It was difficult to give Nandu hope. He left, disconsolate, but checked with us every day, but unfortunately, we had no news for him. Father asked Nandu if Bhiku had left with his suitcase. Yes, he had. For no reason, I felt then that we weren't going to see Bhiku anymore. And we didn't; the only thing that stayed was the memory of an aged man alone in his sadness.

Mr Smith's Treat

Recently a friend told me an anecdote about Fiorello La Guardia who was New York's mayor from 1933 to '45. The story goes that according to La Guardia, the New York police was at times harsher on young offenders than it needed to be. He often said that mischievous pranks and vicious behaviour were two entirely different things. He said that when he was young, he and his friends used to roam the streets and when they found a horse hitched to a post, they untied it, rode it around then brought it back. A policeman asked him, tongue-in-cheek, whether he was saying that the mayor of New York was once a horse thief. No, said La Guardia. What he was saying was that the mayor of New York was once a boy.

On hearing the story, a memory from my school days came back to me. On the way to the town, less than a mile from where we lived, was a house called Rosalynd. It was a beautiful two-storied house, complete with a front garden and a mango orchard at the back. Every day I passed the house on the way to school and on the way back, but I never saw it lived in. The owners did not live in Hazaribagh, and I can't remember if they ever vacationed there either. But Rosalynd never bore a derelict look. It was well kept, its garden was pretty and the orchard was impeccable—no undergrowth or weeds, dry leaves swept clean, the mango trees in a deep cluster, the grounds always spruced and tidy.

The person who managed the property was one whom we knew as Mr Smith. He was an aging man with a tired expression, and he lived alone in his little quarters on the grounds. But he had gentle blue eyes on a tanned, lined face with quiet humour and was never without a genial greeting. I saw him nearly every day going to town on his bicycle for his purchases, or simply biking along the road in front of the house. At other times I saw him supervise the garden.

As his neighbour, I had a comfortable equation with him. Often he invited me over for some sweet, weak tea and tomato sandwiches, which he made while talking to me cheerfully all the while. His room, unlike the house he looked after, could have definitely been tidier. Odds and ends were littered about: torch battery, garden shears, spare bicycle tyre. And books were scattered on the bed, on the chair and on the table. I can still remember some of them: Conan Doyle's *Rodney Stone,* Wilkie Collins's *The Woman in White,* Dickens's *Hard Times,* Thackeray's *Vanity Fair,* and a copy of the Bible.

Mr Smith and I talked of many things. He would talk ramblingly, I would listen and ask questions. I had no idea of his background but I thought he had the tones of a public school. People believed he was perhaps one of the last Englishmen who lived in Hazaribagh. He spoke of the days when Hazaribagh was a great deal quieter and I found this strange since in my time and especially where I lived, Hazaribagh was all about quietude. He spoke of the abundant wildlife in Chhotanagpur country in another time, and he told me how and where one found wild berries, and small sweet dates in the jungle. He spoke of the famous cricket matches; his favourite was the Ashes series. But he never talked about himself. I felt Mr Smith was one of those people who was both known and unknown but I remember with fondness the hours I spent in his company.

There was another good reason why a friend and I took a special interest in Rosalynd—its mango grove. Hazaribagh in those days had houses which were famous for their fruits. A neighbour's house was famous for its guavas, our own house for its 'langra' mangoes. Rosalynd was the envy for its 'bombai' mangoes—big, dark green and delicious. Raiding the Rosalynd grove was a favourite pastime, and we took it up whenever we could. When I let slip this information to my father in a moment of incaution, he reproved severely. What was the point in pilfering from another garden when we had our own? Father, of course, was missing the point entirely; what he didn't see was the joy of the whole experience: the excitement, the fear lest we were caught; the thrill of hide-and-seek in the stillness of the hot afternoon as we furtively scaled the low wall, climbed the trees praying that Mr Smith was asleep in his room, and the sweet rushing relief as we made our way back.

Our piratical expeditions were clearly unknown to Mr Smith, but whenever we ran into him we worried whether he suspected anything at all, and we were always reassured by the good cheer with which he greeted us.

On a Saturday morning when he saw me on my way to school, he invited me and my friend to tea after our classes ended in the afternoon. Coming in from the heat outside, we settled ourselves in the cool comfort of his room. Mr Smith had laid out a treat for us—watermelon juice in jugs, sandwiches (cucumber this time instead of the inevitable tomato), hard-boiled eggs—and we tucked in with undisguised relish. Then came the last treat—a trayful of lovely ripe mangoes from his garden. Mr Smith looked on indulgently and said 'Eat up boys, eat up.' We didn't know how to react and were suddenly filled with embarrassment. Mr Smith told us he had himself picked the mangoes and hoped we would enjoy them. He said pleasantly 'Do tell me whenever you want to sample my mangoes. No need at all for you to climb the wall, scratch yourself over those thorny lantana bushes and take all this trouble. The mangoes are yours for the taking, just let me know and I'll have them picked for you.' We sat shamefaced and guilty, stammered fumbling apologies and slunk away. I'd never again be able to look him in the eye, I told myself.

I needn't have worried too much though as things turned out. A week later, Mr Smith took me on a long cycle ride in the country. We sat under a tree and had a picnic lunch as if nothing had happened. Eventually, in faltering tones I asked him if he was still angry with us that we had raided his mango orchard. 'Don't worry,' he said with a twinkle, 'you wouldn't be boys if you didn't'.

Phuli's Honour

She was thirteen or fourteen, plump and docile and never reacted to censure when she made a mistake, which was rare. Phuli was the daughter of Sukh Ram, who lived in the village. She had no siblings and her parents were her world. Sukh Ram was tall, gaunt and balding. His wife was short, round with chunky trinket jewellery and a face that readily broke into a smile, revealing wide gapped teeth. Phuli's parents were not well-off and life wasn't easy, but they managed. Phuli was the light of their life and they loved her all the more for her nature. She was uncomplaining, quiet and obedient, and devotedly helped her mother with the housework.

The family needed money and Phuli's father sent her to work for a family in the town. The family was only two people, the husband who worked in an office and his wife who kept house. At first things were going generally well for Phuli. She had lots of work to do—sweeping and mopping, washing clothes and hanging them up to dry, grinding spices in the kitchen and washing utensils. The man was neutral, neither kind nor unkind. The wife could be cantankerous but Phuli did not mind her harangues, knowing instinctively that this was the way of some housewives.

Things changed when the family had a guest. She was a distant cousin of the wife, in her forties and single, and was staying for some weeks. Phuli's workload increased but she took it with her usual composure. What upset her was that the cousin was petulant and acrimonious about everything Phuli did—Phuli didn't wash her clothes well, Phuli didn't serve her meals properly, Phuli sulked when asked to do small errands; the complaints never ended. And then strangely, the wife joined in. The husband chose to stay unconnected to the problem and in a week or so his wife and her cousin had made Phuli wretchedly unhappy. They berated and drove her unmercifully.

Sukh Ram guessed that there was something wrong but he kept this from his wife. She of course, as mothers will, knew from her husband's silence that Phuli was in trouble. The last straw fell on a Sunday. It was morning when the cousin announced that her gold earrings were missing. She looked directly at Phuli all the while and then claimed she must have stolen them. The man of the house was reluctant to believe her, but his wife did; if Phuli didn't take them, who else could have?

For the first time Phuli cracked completely. In tearful gasps she told them she had no idea about who had taken the earrings. Desperately she pleaded they believe her, and of course they didn't. The women insisted that Phuli should be handed over to the police. The husband, partly because he had nothing against Phuli and partly because he wanted no involvement with the police, said no. So they turned her out of the house that very morning. Phuli left stoically but when she went home to her parents she broke down, her small body shaking with sobs. Sukh Ram and his wife were bewildered and outraged at the humiliation of their daughter. They went to her employers and implored them to see that Phuli couldn't have stolen the jewellery. They were rebuffed and told to leave.

That, it seemed, was that. Eventually, the cousin returned home. By then husband and wife had begun to feel Phuli's absence—that is in terms of all the work that they now had to manage by themselves, or more specifically by the wife. The man blamed the wife for being hasty because a good housemaid was hard to find. Some days later there was a turn in the situation. Quite by chance, they found the earrings which were lying on the floor at the back of a cupboard. Somehow they had been dropped by accident and in their haste they hadn't searched carefully enough.

Man and wife sat down and thought about it. They now wanted to bring Phuli back and the wife was complaining about all the work she was having to do in the house while her husband spent most of his time away from it. They called Sukh Ram and told him it appeared there may have been a mistake and that in their hearts they had always felt Phuli couldn't have stolen the earrings. All was forgiven and Phuli could come back. Sukh Ram wanted to but couldn't ask them what poor Phuli was being forgiven for. Secretly, he was relieved but he had a favour to ask, he said with the utmost diffidence. His neighbours were whispering that his daughter had committed theft. For him and his wife this was a loss of face in the village and that was too much for them to bear. If he were to bring Phuli to her employers, along with a few elders from the village, could they please set the matter right? Sukh Ram and his wife would be grateful and their mind would then be at peace, as Phuli would be exonerated in the community. The couple, anxious to have Phuli back, agreed, knowing that for these village folk a few specious explanations were going to meet the case.

So a day later, Sukh Ram came to them with Phuli and some village elders. The couple told them matter-of-factly that there had been an unintentional error for which their guest was really responsible. They had always been fond of Phuli and would love to have her back with them. Everyone was relieved, Sukh Ram most of all. The elders murmured among themselves and to him that they had always known there had been a mistake somewhere. And they applauded the couple for their generosity—they were taking Phuli back on a higher wage. All was right with Sukh Ram's world. Gratefully, he smiled at the couple and looked lovingly at his daughter. Things were all right now and Phuli could move in the next day. Phuli, in her calm and placid way, said that she wasn't going back to them—not the next day, not ever. She only wanted that she—once sullied—should now be vindicated in front of the village elders. She was content now to return with her father. Sukh Ram and his friends were incredulous at this turnabout, not seeing that Phuli had turned the humiliation right back to where it came from. The couple were incredulous too, but for young Phuli her ex-employers' expressions of anger and embarrassment were revenge enough.

Tunni and the Flower Arrangement

At age eight Tunni had a kind of mischief and sunniness that surpassed everything else about her. She was skinny all over—skinny frame, skinny arms, skinny legs. She had scraggly hair that looked beyond salvage, and her voice was a thin tenor that was almost shrill. Her mother had died a year ago and Tunni lived with her father who was an itinerant worker. Overburdened by the daily tightrope of earning whatever he could from place to place, he finally gave up on raising his daughter. So he did the sensible thing; he implored the middle-aged couple who led quiet lives in their town to take his daughter in. He often did odd repair jobs in their home and when he explained his plight the couple agreed to take in Tunni to work for them. Of work there was virtually none. Tunni lived with the couple and wasn't required to do anything beyond the occasional dusting and helping in the kitchen. The housework was actually done by the wife herself and the maid who came in twice a day.

The reason why the couple took in Tunni was simple. They were lonely, their son and daughter lived away from Hazaribagh with families of their own. And they adored Tunni for her perpetual cheerfulness and her total lack of self-pity. She was like a breeze in their placid lives and despite her difficult childhood, Tunni reminded me of Browning's Pippa as she looked only at the bright side of things. Once, running out into the rain she tripped and hurt her foot. When scolded for recklessness she said she enjoyed running in the rain. Another time, in a reverse situation she was excited about the shopping trip her guardians promised to take her on. Before they could leave, rain started coming down and the trip had to be called off. Tunni was not disappointed; she said it was fun listening to the rain drumming on the window panes—something she couldn't enjoy outdoors.

But mischief was Tunni's special gift. One look at her and you could tell she was up to something, and she had variety. She took out the ink from the inkwell and replaced it with water. She put salt instead of sugar in the tea. She put a frog on her guardians' bed. She hid a shoe from each pair they wore. But the more mischief she did, the more affection flowed out of them and extreme cases earned her only a mild scolding.

By now Tunni's employers had assumed the position of surrogate parents, treating her as one of their own. Tunni was beginning to lose her skinniness, and her hair, through the patient care of her new mother, was no longer scraggly—it didn't shine yet, but had become straighter and thicker.

Although Tunni knew her alphabet, she had no use for books. She was put in a girls' school but ignored the insistence on studies. She was happiest in the house where she was inseparable from her new parents. She disliked classes and the other girls disliked her for her antics.

On a day in March, the school organized a flower

arrangement contest. Curiously, Tunni talked about it all the time. When asked if she was interested, she vigorously denied it. But the contest had caught her fancy somehow. After a great deal of persuasion, she agreed to participate. The date of the contest came around and a good many children came to the school hall to show what they could do. Without exception, all of them made attractive displays of flowers, ferns and leaves in careful and symmetrical arrangements which drew admiring looks. Tunni came in late, bringing only a few things with her. She brought a shallow oval wooden bowl which she had cleaned and polished, some large glossy banyan leaves and a cluster of small red roses. She first placed the leaves in the tray so that they completely covered its base and spilled over the edges. Then she scattered the blood-red roses on the leaves, no pattern to them at all. The whole thing took only a few minutes, but the result, to say the least, was dramatic.

It was now judging time. The three judges were full of praise for all the efforts that the girls had put in, and had a special word for Tunni's creation, with its artless contrast between the rich green leaves and the vibrant red roses. It was simply beautiful, they said. The other girls and their parents who had nothing but derision for Tunni—a girl who had no experience of flowers or trees when she was a small child—watched in angry disbelief as she took the prize for best display.

Haria's Loss

He was Haria, he said when I asked his name one day. He was no more than eight or nine, and he tended to his father's cows. It was early September, the fields green after the monsoon rains, the weather softening, already turning mellow, autumn just ahead. On the fields around our house cattle grazed, shepherd boys in tow, and Haria was one of them. He was a quiet boy but cheerful, and at peace with himself. I never could help a smile as I often saw him struggling to get on the back of one of his cows which waited patiently till Haria managed to climb up before it started on its slow, leisurely amble.

The afternoon with its sounds had a typical ambience. The first was the flute which Haria and some of the other boys played, sitting on their animals. It was oddly shaped—oval—made out of clay with blowholes and gave off the curiously hollow, sweet woodwind notes. The other was the cow bells. These were made of wood, and their 'tap-tap' sounds had a peculiar ring to them. The sleepy cadence of the flutes merged easily with the cow bell tinkles and the two gave the still afternoons a wonderfully lazy temper.

Haria on his cow's back, playing his flute and watching over his small herd was something I saw every day. My attraction though was watching him with his favourite, the baby of the herd. A few weeks old, she was inseparable from her mother on the fields. And Haria was inseparable from the little calf. The calf was irresistible. She was around the size of a very large sheepdog, had an uncertain gait, a coat of milk white, a gentle face with the most beautiful dark, limpid eyes you ever saw.

Haria couldn't bear to be away from this calf he adored, never letting her out of his sight. It was touching, the way he looked after her. If she looked tired, Haria brought her grass. He instinctively knew when she was thirsty and brought her water to drink. And the calf was equally fond of Haria. She came to him without being called and sometimes gently and playfully butted him on the chest and Haria loved it. Many times he sat with his arms around her, lying on the grass, whispering to her in soft tones and nuzzling her neck. Sometimes he played his flute to her while she stood still; whether Haria's playing mattered at all to her was of course something only he knew. But they got along splendidly, as true friends will.

The mellow autumn days slipped into each other, slow and torpid and Haria and his calf became an everyday sight. I once asked him by what name he called her and he looked puzzled. He didn't call her by any name at all, he said. She came to him when she wanted to. This clearly was a very special friendship.

Then one day something tragic happened. Haria's calf had somehow strayed from her barn at night and a predator took her. Most likely it was a hungry leopard on the prowl. They found her some distance away, or rather they found what was left of her. Haria's grief when he saw the pitiful carcass was terrible to see, his father told my parents. His cry was visceral. It was heart-wrenching and it went on and on. The villagers became nervous at the almost unnatural intensity of it all; not their fault, of course, because they could not have known how much this calf meant to Haria, this vulnerable little animal that was his companion in those lonely days on the grazing fields.

Haria stopped shepherding his father's cattle. His father, his heart going out to his son, coaxed and pleaded but Haria refused to spend his days with the herd. His father hired a boy from the village till the situation improved. For days things stayed this way till Haria's father told his son that he could not afford the arrangement any longer. Realizing he had no choice in the matter, Haria had to look after the herd. So Haria was back with his cows on the fields. He looked much the same as before. He looked after the cows, kept them from straying and brought them back home safe at sundown. But he was no more his old self. He was silent when the cows grazed and he no longer played his little flute that was so much a part of the afternoon mood. I asked him one day to play it and he said outright he didn't want to. When I tried to talk to him he made it clear he didn't want to talk. This was a long way off from someone who once chatted with me easily. Other flutes sounded, but not Haria's and that made a difference. Over the weeks my memory of that poor calf was kept distressingly alive whenever I saw Haria. He was withdrawn and silent. I wondered how many boys would have suffered as he was suffering, and the scars he carried were beyond me. Could it be that he blamed himself for letting the calf stray? He didn't say what was going on in his mind but I knew no one could possibly guess the kind of pain that was his.

It was nearly a month and Haria's grief wasn't showing the slightest sign of thawing. One day someone in his village had an idea to get Haria out of his state of constant despair. He gave Haria one of the pups the village dog had given birth to. The little puppy had all the appeal of his species—plump, brown patches on white, a happy face that looked up trustingly. We knew Haria's life was now going to be better. The puppy took to Haria at once, following him around all the time, coming to him, his little tail waggling busily and always wanting a snuggle. The two grew close together slowly, and it was almost imperceptible. Haria seemed glad to have the dog and sometimes played with it. This pleased everyone. Days passed but Haria still didn't play his flute. I spoke to my father and he said that 'a boy and his dog' was a sure therapy which simply couldn't go wrong, and it wouldn't be much longer before Haria went back to his old, contented ways. One afternoon—it was around mid-October—we saw Haria on the back of his cow, playing the flute. My father gave me an 'I told you so' look. But I could sense that something wasn't right. Haria's flute didn't sound quite the same, by which I mean that it seemed to be without the peacefulness it once had, and it sounded desultory and forced.

There was something else, and it had to do with the puppy. Puzzlingly, Haria's earlier closeness with it seemed to have cooled. The puppy was as devoted as it always had been but Haria, though fond of it, looked strangely restrained. It was clear. I saw the puppy one day eagerly trotting toward Haria. It went up to him, lay down by his side, rolled on its back and looked up, expecting his stomach to be scratched. Haria patted its head, almost absent minded and casual and that was all. It was almost a rejection, unintended perhaps but a rejection all the same. The puppy persisted, uncomprehending yet hopeful, but Haria was really far away. I couldn't know if the dog felt the indifference; very possibly it did. But something was missing between the both of them and perhaps this explained why the puppy was seen less and less with Haria; when they were together, it looked almost like a neutral companionship.

It was clear to me now. Haria after all hadn't got over his beloved calf. Whether of his own choosing or against it, he stayed within the prison of his sadness. Not the passing of days, not the loyalty of the friendly little puppy, not the concern of his parents could bring him back. Something had emptied out of him and the child in Haria was gone.

A Milkman's Son

The quiet of the morning was broken by a sudden clatter, and it came from the empty cans the milkmen carried on their cycles as they rode back to their village after making their deliveries in town. This was a regular scene on the roads in the mornings.

On the way back from town, the road dipped very steeply and then levelled out a little way from our gate. On this stretch cycles were not pedalled, most times cars rolled down in neutral gear and drivers had a difficult time checking their speed. One summer morning I heard the familiar mix of sounds from some returning milkmen—their loud and jovial conversation, their songs that came out in sudden yells, the whirr of their cycles and the unmistakable clanking of the milk cans. Suddenly something went wrong. One of the cycles had gone out of control on the downslope. The rider and the boy with him went rolling on the ground, and the cycle, lying on its side, wheels still spinning, looked like a crippled animal. There was immediate consternation, the man and the boy got up shakily. They were unhurt, save for some scratches. The reason for this little accident was that the handle bar had gone askew, a common occurrence and easily set right.

The owner lifted his cycle, went to the front of it and held the front wheel tightly between his knees. He then held the handle bar firmly and pulled it back to its original position. The cycle was ready to go, but would need some looking into. During this whole exercise, that took no more than about fifteen minutes, the man's fellow riders waited patiently, but the little boy had got my attention.

I judged him to be no more than thirteen or fourteen years old and he was the cyclist's son. My first impressions were decidedly unpleasant. The boy was short for his age and had a dourness on his face the whole time he waited for his father to fix the cycle. Repair over, the little group came to our house, the man and his son washed up at our well before setting off again for their home in the village, which we were told was a little more than a mile away.

By then it was clear that the scowl on the boy's face was a fixed feature and the owner of this face was a permanently surly individual. It showed in the way he behaved with his father, and it showed in the way he reacted towards the others who showed concern when he had the little accident. Our household help, who was from the same village where the milkman lived, said he knew the family well. He said Kanua—that was the boy's name—was easily the most detested youngster in the village, and I had no problem believing him. For no accountable reason, Kanua was unvaryingly unpleasant towards all, and anyone coming in contact with him was sure to be a recipient of his even-handed rudeness. The catalogue of his misdemeanours ran long and unrelieved. A neighbouring villager called on Kanua's father and true to his nature Kanua told him to go away—he didn't even bother to check with his father. Kanua's older brother once asked for his help in moving a bale of hay. Kanua asked him to do it himself. When Kanua's father asked him to bring the cycle around, he simply walked away. An unsuspecting boy in the village asked Kanua if he would like to play marbles with him—Kanua shooed him off. Even the village elders were exasperated by his rudeness. Everybody in the village wondered at this aberration, but Kanua didn't seem to care. It wasn't that Kanua was a loner, only that he carried an unhappy chip on his shoulder.

It was on an afternoon late in summer when something unusual happened. A bullock cart with some men in it was on its way home along a lonely stretch of road. In the fierce heat of day, dust storm blowing, the men saw something in the distance. It was a man. He was aged and frail and he was lying by the roadside, weak and helpless. Clearly the heat had got the better of him and, exhausted, he had collapsed. Beside the old man was a boy and he was vainly trying to drag the man to the shade under a tree. The men in the approaching cart could make out that the boy was gesticulating at them. And from the distance, through the driving wind and dust, his shrill and desperate cries for help came repeatedly.

The bullock cart stopped, and the old man was helped in it, joined by the boy. The boy was Kanua. Quite by chance he had seen the old man lying by the roadside, and futilely he had been trying to get the man away from the cruel heat from the sun.

The man was going home to his village. What was inexplicable was Kanua's role in the incident. Why had he acted in a way totally contrary to his nature? Why did he do this unexpected and untypical thing? What was it that had moved him to reach out to a helpless old man? Was this a sign that he was changing after all? He wasn't and he was back again to his churlish self. Our household help, who told us of this incident, was baffled. And he wasn't the only one.

BIRDS OF PASSAGE

Author, Author

He was much more than an author. As he often put it himself, he was really a man of many attributes, an important one of which—besides his renown as a writer—was that he was a zealous fighter of crime, soldiering on against thieves and robbers. Something he kept low key and few people knew about.

One winter, a neighbour's house was host to a group of vacationers. This beautiful home was the property of a family from Calcutta whom we saw about once or twice a year when they spent a couple of weeks in Hazaribagh. The group—friends of the family—could not have come at a better time. The bracing winter of Hazaribagh was always a balm for body and soul, and in this group were our author and his wife.

Our author (henceforth simply referred to as Author) had already made a name as a Bengali novelist, his latest book winning stirring acclaim among readers and critics, and he intended to use his Hazaribagh sojourn as fuel for inspiration for his next novel. Author's appearance was strikingly aquiline. With us youngsters (the daughter of the visiting family and I), he was invariably taciturn, as if we were a bothersome presence. I was properly reverential whenever I was near him.

He spent long hours at our house in conversation with my parents and my elder brother, and whenever I could, I tried to listen in. All were keen to discuss the book that had brought him accolades. They wanted to know about the book that he was working on. His response was always vague and evasive, as though he felt that it was commonplace to be admired by everybody, and that could only mean a lowering of his standards. His calm pronouncement was that his audience belonged to the 'intellectual set'.

Sometimes we would go to the countryside on picnics and the locations varied. It could be a shady sal grove on a meadow, or it could be beside a gentle, shallow waterfall. Another time it could be a green grassy slope beside a stream. I was certain that like the rest of us, Author enjoyed these outings, but it was difficult to tell since he kept to himself, contemplating, as someone said admiringly, his next work.

The only time Author became animated—so far as this was possible—was when conversation touched on crime and investigation. Author told us that not many knew of his proficiency in this particular field. He informed us that he was a 'committed soldier' who disliked criminals and was ready to join the fray in stopping them, whether or not he was in the throes of literary composition. His father had been a senior official in the police force and thus his initiation in the complex game of crime detection and prevention had begun early. Wasn't this obsession unusual for a writer? he was asked. With unaffected aplomb he said that he was an artist and as an artist he could not tolerate any threat to or disruption in the normal rhythm of life. His track record here was a long one, he said. One in which he had done detective work, complete with laying traps and wading into the thick of the action regardless of the risk involved. He proceeded to run through a quick catalogue of his exploits, mostly in and around Calcutta and at any time of the day or night.

His principal targets, he said, were burglars and he talked about those he had caught—or helped catch—in the act. The secret, he said, was to be totally unafraid, giving us a neat example. If in a rough-and-tumble football match you're afraid of getting hurt, chances are you will end up getting hurt, he told us. When Author recounted his feats, he did it without any bravado whatsoever, narrating all that he did and how he went about it as if these were little more than a day-in-the-life. We listened agog.

One evening after Author had left, I kept going back to what he said about 'soldiering on' against criminals. My father said with a straight face that Author belonged to the tradition of great novelists who were also soldiers. Cervantes, he reminded me, fought in the battle of Lepanto. Of course the battlefields were different. Cervantes was fighting the Ottoman Turks, while Author was fighting the enemy within. But both were soldiers. I looked closely at Father to detect the humour I knew was there, but he gave nothing away.

Author's story ended like this: There was a strong buzz that one of the most dangerously notorious criminals in the area—known as Jabbu Ram—had escaped prison and the police were in hot pursuit of him. Jabbu Ram had a list of horrifying crimes to his name: robbery, theft, extortion and infliction of serious bodily harm were some of them. Both townsfolk and villagers were terrified of him, and the air was tense, something rare for Hazaribagh in those days.

Around this time the visiting family returned to Calcutta. Author's wife also left and he was set to follow in a few days. Since he was now alone, he asked my brother to spend a few nights with him. He would be glad of the company, he said, after the whole day by himself. So my brother was off to our neighbour's house with Author.

Their first two nights passed uneventfully. The third night brought the change. In the cold winter night both Author and my brother turned in early for bed, everything quiet in and around the house. A little after midnight they were shaken awake by the almost hysterical caretaker who was unintelligible in his excitement and alarm. What he managed to get across was this: looking for shelter from the cold, Jabbu Ram was holed up in the house. He had entered one of the rooms, waiting for morning, and unfortunately for him, he had dozed off. With reckless courage the caretaker had locked the door from the outside and alerted some men living close by. What now? he asked.

The threat of Jabbu Ram had reached its end. The man was locked in a room and all that needed to be done was to call the police to pick him up. This was the sane advice my brother put forward. A simple solution really, but Author had a different idea. He declared rather grandly that there was nothing laudable in putting the cuffs on a criminal unable to defend himself. He instructed the caretaker's friends to stand by. Getting hold of a sturdy stick, he asked the caretaker to unlock the door. He would then overpower the criminal man to man and hand him over to the police himself. He brusquely brushed aside all opposition to this ludicrous idea and stood ready. The caretaker, having no option, did as he was told. And very sensibly my brother, knowing it was futile to argue, rushed to the phone to call the police. Several things happened after that. When the caretaker unbolted the door, Jabbu Ram, furious at being locked in, screamed in rage and rushed out. The sundry helpers, terror stricken, bolted. The caretaker stood a distance away, cowering. And Author, at the sight of Jabbu Ram coming what he thought was straight for him, took a few staggering steps back, slumped heavily to the ground, his stick falling away, and stayed prone, completely unmoving. Jabbu Ram, in full command of the situation, totally ignored Author, walked across to the boundary wall, scaled it in one effortless leap and was gone. The Police arrived too late to do anything.

Well before daybreak Author packed his suitcase, left his host's home and came to ours. The whole story came from my brother. In the morning Author said he had some work in town. This, we came to know afterwards, was going to the petrol station to fill up his car. He returned shortly and after a quick goodbye, hurried his driver to get behind the wheel and drove away rapidly for Calcutta, home and safety.

Hunting Party

'They are coming this Sunday,' my father said as he passed the letter across to me. It was from a distant relative in Calcutta—a businessman—saying that his son and the son's friend would be staying with us in Hazaribagh on a couple of weeks' vacation. We normally had guests during this time of year because autumn was much loved by vacationers. This was understandable because autumn through winter to spring were a marvellous time in Hazaribagh when the weather was at its finest: mellow turning to sharp cold to spring's warmth.

Our friends chose October for another reason, as I found out later. They came on a Sunday afternoon, driving up from Calcutta. Probir, the son, was in his mid-twenties like his friend Debu. I was no more than fifteen then, but I could sense in them a barely disguised air of condescension, as though their presence were a favour conferred on us. My parents' spontaneous—not to mention elaborate—hospitality was received with a cool casualness. I recall a conversation the day after they came. Their room had all the comforts one could ask for, and it looked out onto a lovely field and the hills beyond it. Father asked them if they liked the room and the view, to which they said indifferently that it would have to do. There was also the incident of the stray dog which often came to the house for food. One morning we heard him cry out in pain. Mother and I rushed out to check. Debu had hit him with a piece of rock and was standing there, grinning. 'What a marksman,' Mother said bitterly.

Two days into their stay, Probir and Debu asked with nonchalant bravado what game was available for hunting. Neither my parents nor I cared about hunting, and we kept our shotgun strictly for protection. Father's face clouded over and his annoyance was clear, as was Mother's. In an attempt at irony, Father told them he would try and see if he could gather round a few obliging rhinos who would be willing to set themselves up for our visitors' benefit. The humour was lost. Sapiently, Probir and Debu proceeded to inform us that there were no rhinos in Hazaribagh, and since we lived there, surely we should have known? They were 'shikaris' they said, and knew about the wilds. Probir also showed us the gun licence he was carrying. They had come to Hazaribagh because October was supposed to be good hunting season. Reluctantly, Father gave in and lent him the gun; but insisted I go with them. And then he said something quite amusing. He asked if I could make sure that 'they didn't get anything'. How I was going to manage that, I had no idea. Could warning the animal away help? he suggested. As it turned out, Father need not have worried at all.

Hunting Trip 1

We set out in the afternoon for the forest which was about ten miles away, where shoots were allowed. There were four of us: Probir, Debu, my friend Ashok who was visiting and lived close by, and I. When the two from Calcutta turned up for the journey, we smiled in spite of ourselves at the sheer comicality of it all. They were dressed for the part—khaki trousers, khaki hunting shirts with shoulder straps and wide-brimmed hats.

Their car was parked by the roadside and the driver was waiting. We entered the forest which grew thicker as we walked, till the forest floor was full of undergrowth. For a better field of view, we climbed up two spreading trees—Probir and Ashok in one, Debu and I on the one next to it. Much to Debu's indignation, I didn't give him the gun, keeping it strapped to my shoulder. The forest was quiet, only the somnolent call of a bird somewhere. With the gravitas of the hunter, Probir warned that we must make absolutely no sound. Time passed, but no animal came in sight.

Suddenly, with a shrill cry Debu slithered down the branches, falling heavily to the ground. We clambered down. He had multiple scratches on his face and his ankle was already beginning to swell. We carried him to the car and headed home.

My parents were all concern. The cuts were cared for, and the swelling was treated with hot and cold compresses. We asked him later why he had panicked and what we gathered was the following: On the tree, he had felt something crawl down his neck. With the shikari's instinct he knew at once that this was a snake, which was why he lost his nerve. It could happen to anybody, he said. I knew better, as I was beside him the whole time and had felt the same thing. It wasn't a snake at all. It was a leaf brushing against his neck in the soft breeze.

Hunting Trip 2

The next day, Debu the shikari was much better, but ceased to take any further interest in the proceedings. What he had really come for, he confided to us, was rest.

This did not deter the dauntless Probir. He insisted we drive back to the forest, and off we went in the late afternoon—Probir, Ashok and I. This time we did not venture deep into the forest and kept close to the edge. We did see a small bear, but before our hunter could react, Ashok and I chased it away. We found nothing else, and by the time we came out from the forest edge, it was already dark, and we still had a good fifteen minutes' walk to the car. Walking along the side of the narrow road, we saw something—a pair of eyes glowing in the dark. Ashok and I were familiar with this, but not our latter-day Corbett. It was only a wandering cow looking for its keeper, and then it mooed, a searching call. Probir, of course, could not hear it. He had fainted.

Hunting Trip 3

The previous night's experience left Probir completely unperturbed, but only after hearing about the cow. 'It's nothing really,' he said with airy dismissal. He insisted we go back again, but both Ashok and I had had enough. So we settled for a wooded area about three miles away. Probir demanded that he 'handle the shoot' and carried the gun. In the afternoon light we saw a tree with large ring-necked doves perched on its branches. Probir crouched into position, aimed and fired. He did not disappoint. Instantly, there was a flurry of wings as the birds took off. But Probir was on the ground, his nose bloodied, and he was moaning in pain. The gun was a 12-gauge double-barrelled Walter Locke with twin hammers. Our shikari had obviously held the stock at a wrong angle against his shoulder. The recoil made the breech block and sent the hammers slamming into his nose. So ended the third and final hunt.

My parents—Mother mostly—were beside themselves with consternation. The doctor was called, bandages properly applied, and for the night and the next day, Probir had to manage on a liquid diet.

Around the seventh day of their stay, Probir announced that they must drive back for Calcutta the next morning, as he was needed urgently at home. My parents were disappointed, but I was secretly gleeful.

The next morning Probir and Debu prepared to drive back after breakfast, with a sumptuous lunch and dinner packed for the way. A little more poetic justice still remained. Probir, shaken by his ordeal, and Debu, still wobbly on his feet, started for the car at the driveway. Along their way, the stray dog lay quietly on the side. At the sound of their footsteps, the stray got up and chased them, barking furiously. The duo, hobbling and panting, managed to get to the safety of their car which drove out of our gate. I imagined fondly that this was the final disincentive that propelled our brave shikaris enthusiastically on their way.

Night Halt

The rain that came that late May evening was unmistakably a nor'wester, given that it was still not early monsoon. The sky darkened quickly to ink-black, then came howling, swirling winds, sheets of slashing rain and total darkness, and staying indoors gave a wonderful feeling of safety.

The car horn in the distance was muffled but insistent and I stepped out to the verandah for a look. Outside our gate, by the side of the road, appeared the dim outline of a car, and I still remember it was a Hillman. Someone came out, torch in hand and he played the beam in an arc to feel his way about. We asked him in from the rain and by that time he was nearly all wet. Once inside we had a clear view of him. The man in front of us was around middle age and had a large, honest face, and his hair was grey at the temples. It would have been a friendly face, but for the dour look he had about him. It wasn't that he was churlish, only that he wasn't inviting any conversation. Very courteously he asked if it would be too much trouble to put him up for the night. His car had broken down and his driver was going to sleep in the car till it could be repaired in the morning. My father remonstrated, saying we could easily put him up as well; one look from our visitor was signal enough that here was a man who did not brook argument, and that was that.

That he was a distinguished and successful person was evident. During dinner he was mostly silent, courteous in his replies to what my parents asked him—where he was from, what he did, simple routine stuff. But he hardly spoke until spoken to. He didn't even ask us the basics that made for conversation—our life in Hazaribagh, the school I went to, and so on. What an unlikeable man, I thought.

The little we could gather from him was this: He ran a prosperous business in Kolkata (no details of what and where) and had driven up to Ranchi on work. From Ranchi he planned to drive to Patna to meet up with his wife and son who were staying there on a brief vacation, and then the family would return to Calcutta. But something inescapable had come up, he told us tersely that made him leave Ranchi straightaway for Patna. His manner seemed to say: 'I have told you all that you needed to know. Don't ask me anything more.'

Dinner was completed in near silence and as the driver had also finished his meal, our visitor said quietly that he wished to turn in for the night. I'm certain that my parents—used to traditional courtesy—would have been somewhat disappointed, because he had not troubled to thank them, even casually, for their hospitality. The real reason why they were a little saddened of course was that they loved company, and this person certainly wasn't that.

The rain had spent itself out during the night and morning broke clear and sunny. After his breakfast, the driver went to the town to fetch a mechanic. The rest of us lingered over our breakfast with our guest, and the conversation, to put it mildly, was desultory. True to form, he was withdrawn, almost impatient with all the attention he was getting. Finally, the mechanic arrived on his bicycle and our guest went up to the car to see to the repairs. It took a good couple of hours before the Hillman was ready to roll.

My mother had put lunch boxes in the car to sustain them on the way and this was received with no more than a perfunctory acknowledgement, and by now I was becoming tired of his presence. Travellers along the highway stopping at our place for the day was not an uncommon occurrence. But this man, who had been looked after with such care, and who had spent the night at our home, was one of a kind. No matter how courteous he seemed, it was a rigid kind of courtesy that seemed graceless.

It was time at last for our guest to leave. We gathered round to say goodbye. Our visitor came up to my parents, and for the first time, I thought I saw something close to a softening in his expression. He sincerely apologized for having failed to show appreciation for helping him and his driver when they were stranded. This troubled him a great deal, he said and also the fact that he had been unable to do anything about it. He said quite uncharacteristically that this was the darkest time of his life. The reason he had cut short his stay in Ranchi and was hurrying back to Patna was that his son—fourteen years old and his only child—had died in an accident the day before. His wife had gone into shock. He didn't want to trouble us with this news and could my parents please excuse him if his behaviour was unworthy? He said this with a kind of grim reserve, trying not to break down, and in a moment this man who only the evening before had seemed cold and unapproachable had changed into one crushed by grief and circumstance. Stunned, my parents reached out to him, and in their instinctive sympathy told him stammeringly how truly sorry they were. It was a totally inadequate gesture, for standing there bewildered and broken, this man was beyond any sharing of pain. Without another word he got into his car and drove away.

Last Laugh

'We've got a guest in the house. He's come with us from Calcutta for a vacation in Hazaribagh,' said the owner of the house which was about two miles away from ours and in the opposite direction. But in Hazaribagh of those days, distance didn't really matter and everyone we knew were our neighbours, irrespective of where they stayed. I passed this spacious bungalow whenever I walked or cycled to Canary Hill, lovely in its setting in the deeply wooded country. The owner and his family came to Hazaribagh about once a year after the summer months. This family and my own visited each other's homes when they were in Hazaribagh and that's how I met the guest. My neighbour described him—Manoj—as 'a very likeable lad' and was certain that I would get along with him. I wasn't disappointed. He was around my age, friendly enough in a quiet sort of way, and we got on fairly well mainly because some of our interests converged. He admired Conan Doyle, Dickens and Kipling and so did I. He loved rock 'n' roll and folk as I did and often we spent time talking about passages from our favourite books or tunes from music.

Visitors from Calcutta, or for that matter any large city, loved going on walks. What amused me invariably was the way many of them went about it. They walked as though they were on an assignment that had to be completed in a no-nonsense way. They walked with a kind of grim determination—eyes straight ahead, steps a lot faster than brisk, no talking, silent and purposeful. It was all hilarious. This was how my neighbour and his sons took their walks and they were irked by Manoj's refusal to join them. It was the same when the two brothers went cycling. He detested the speed the two obviously enjoyed and stayed away. His routine was the precise opposite. He enjoyed strolling in the large garden. He loved sitting there in the afternoons until the sun dipped behind the hills. And when he walked—which was mostly in my company—he actually ambled, stopping now and then to check on some wild flower. He looked up at the trees, watching the play of leaves and light, and he frequently crushed eucalyptus leaves between his fingers to breathe in their smell.

His laid-back nature and seeming laziness made him the object of raillery which sometimes verged on plain ridicule. The two boys of the family never let slip the smallest opportunity. 'Are you rested enough, Manoj?' one would ask. The other would say, 'Did you drink your milk this morning?' Even the caretaker's son, younger than the rest of us, ribbed, 'Can you get to the gate on your own?' Manoj took these taunts with a serene indifference that was remarkable for his age and he never reacted. The gibes continued and I confess with a sense of guilt that now and then I joined in the banter, telling myself that this was all good-natured fun.

We decided that our 'very likeable lad' was simply lazy. Didn't he play games in school? He answered yes.

Didn't he like the outdoors? Oh yes, he did, very much, he assured us. When I was alone with him one day, I suggested he should fall in with others' wishes, meaning of course the family he'd come with, since they were disappointed with his attitude. His answer was that he was enjoying himself and running about wasn't always his idea of a good time; he couldn't help it if he had let the family down. Hearing him talk, he sounded like a wise old man.

One of our regular enterprises was walking to Canary Hill, close to where Manoj was staying. Our favourite pastime was to climb up this small hill from the shorter side. It was no trouble clambering over boulders or branches till we reached the top. One day we persuaded Manoj to come with us. There were four of us—the two brothers, he and I. Upon reaching Canary Hill, we set up a simple contest to see who could get to the top first. We asked Manoj to stay back and wait for us but oddly he said he wanted to take part, rather than being alone at the foot of the hill. This, to say the least, was a surprise. There was more. He said he would like to try the longer side of the hill, not the short one that we always took. It dawned upon us then—this was his turn for teasing us. We smiled knowingly, left him standing there and started up, scaling the smallest boulders within reach and using the branches that gave us support and leverage. The three of us finally reached the top, rumpled and sweaty but feeling wonderfully alive. In the cold, sharp air we stood catching our breaths, and then we saw Manoj standing a little way from us. We gaped open-mouthed. He had taken the longer route up and yet reached before us! That was plainly absurd and simply didn't add up. Manoj broke the silence and asked what had kept us; he had been waiting for us to show up.

Chastened and disbelieving, we made our way down. None of us spoke and we grappled with this reversal from all earlier situations when Manoj was the silent butt of our jokes. And in the confusion we were in, it was hard to make out what had got the better of us; was it the fact that we'd been led on? Or was it that the whole incident was beyond belief? Manoj, being the 'very likeable lad' he was, didn't say anything, of course. He offered no explanation and acted as if nothing had happened. But the hard truth was that he had bested us and what made it worse was he refused to boast about it.

The next day I asked him fumblingly how he had managed the climb, and along a much tougher route, at that. Oh, didn't he tell us? he asked. He must have forgotten, he said carelessly. He belonged to some club in Calcutta that did trekking expeditions in tough, hilly terrains.

Stranger at the Hill

Roughly five miles away from town, down a long stretch of tree-shaded winding road stands Canary Hill, a Hazaribagh icon. On either side of the road that took you to the hill were stately homes, imposing and silent since the owners, mostly families from Calcutta, vacationed here once or twice a year but not more than that. After you passed the last house—a large, imperious structure called Gibraltar—the road continued its way, reaching Canary Hill.

It was curious that Canary Hill should have qualified as one of Hazaribagh's two major landmarks, the other being the town's lake. At first glance, Canary Hill was hardly impressive; it wasn't high and was almost nondescript, but its appeal was undeniable. Set amid thick woods, it was astonishingly picturesque, and the surrounding silence provided a deep and rare restfulness to both visitors and locals like myself. The name Canary, as per popular lore, is derived from 'Kanheri', reportedly meaning 'bow-and-arrow shaped' in the local dialect, though I could never tell the similarity.

Canary Hill lifted easily to the sky and was clearly visible for miles around. Nearly every weekend I took lonely walks there. Most times I hiked cross-country across the fields and slopes behind our house, a distance of about a mile. At other times I took the longer way, cycling along the quiet road that led to it. Clambering up to the hill, at least part of the way, or simply walking through the serene woods was pure pleasure.

One afternoon when we were indoors, there came a muffled but unmistakable sound of explosion from across the hill and the suddenness of it was startling. After some minutes came the sound of another explosion and then another. The Forest Department was dynamiting the hill, clearing rocks and trees to make a commutable road from the base to the top, where it proposed to build a small guest house. For days we could hear the booming and disturbing sounds of dynamite going off. My father told me categorically that I was not to go near the hill until the work was completed.

And so it went, days of unceasing detonations which sometimes started forest fires that we could see from our courtyard and garden—flames coursing up the side of the hill like an angry, living thing. Finally, the detonations stopped and the road-laying work began. Once this was finished, the construction of the guest house started. By the time autumn came around, the entire project was completed.

It was exciting to go to the new Canary Hill, with the road going up all the way to the guest house perched on the peak. The forest department had cleared away all the debris—rocks, boulders, felled trees—and the place was again quiet and inviting. I resumed my trips on days it didn't rain and with the coming of autumn, spent my afternoons in the woodland more regularly. And I enjoyed taking the road up the hill, something

I did often. The curve along the hillside had its own beauty: the silence was total, the rest of the world seemed far away, and the depth of the trees on either side gave one the feeling of being completely enclosed. The best part was when you reached the top. From the observation point, the view of the landscape below was dramatic. You had the entire sweep of the countryside: fields and meadows, small farmed patches, groves and hedges, breaks and dips in the ground, the whole view as though in miniature. In full moonlight, the view was unforgettable.

In the days before the road was built, I often came across a man on my walks. I went at all times depending on when it was possible, but I saw him mainly on winter afternoons. The first time I saw him he was he was sitting on a small boulder by some trees, a curiously solitary figure.

He acknowledged me with a quiet nod—no smile—and I found myself in conversation with him, except that to call it a conversation was stretching the term. The little he said was in English and I guessed he was not a local; if he were he would have almost certainly used Hindi.

The man was past middle age, serious and distinguished looking, and his diction was clear. The little I could gather was that he was from Patna, had retired and was living alone. Every year he spent the autumn and winter months with a relative in Hazaribagh. I didn't dare ask anything more and it did not occur to me to ask him his age. But clearly he was a man of education. On his part, he asked me nothing except where I lived and where I studied. Oddly, we grew to be somewhat companionable, and on most afternoons we met at the hill, I falling in step with him and walking in companionable silence. The two of us enjoyed the little things that defined the mood of the place: the dappled light through the trees, the faint rustle of a squirrel or rabbit as it scurried along the dry leaves, the call of a dove somewhere in the distance, a startled fox running away. After our walk we returned, he towards the town where he stayed and I the opposite way towards home.

One winter I did not see the stranger on my walks and was sorry to miss his company on the woodland trail. It was the time of our annual school holidays, a span of six weeks or so when I found myself at Canary Hill on most afternoons; but he never showed up. I had nearly given up on him, thinking he wasn't coming to Hazaribagh after all. Then one day I saw him on the road to the town market. I asked him why he no longer came to the hill. He didn't want to talk about it at first, but gradually opened up. Arriving in Hazaribagh he had walked to his haunt that he loved so much. What he saw, he said, repelled him. The lovely little hill and the tranquil woods were no longer as he remembered them. All he saw was the road along the hill which looked like a hideous wound, and gave way to the guest house, which even from that distance looked ugly and out of place. This was a terrible violation and his hours of peace at the hill were over. Which was why he couldn't bear to come to Canary Hill anymore.

He wasn't making any sense to me, and I told him that Canary Hill was now a great favourite with visitors. Besides, what could be his objection to the road up the hill? Didn't mountain passes have miles and miles of road? Winding roads came naturally on high passes, he said, and not on a small hill sitting peaceably by itself. There was no case for invading its tranquility. He also added that the construction work was bound to have frightened the wildlife away.

This was patently absurd and he was making far too much of this. I tried to tell him that this little project was certainly an improvement for the viewers' delight. 'Improvement over what?' he asked in disdain, and why on earth couldn't they leave this place alone? For the first time I felt a rush of irritation with the man, quite simply because he was so hopelessly hidebound. Suddenly, I wasn't enjoying his company any more. There was no real merit in what he said and I saw him for what he was—unreasonable and biased beyond salvage. But I tried one more time. Would he, for my sake, walk with me to the hill top? The view was sure to reduce his prejudice. He refused at first but finally gave in.

On the appointed day—it was late morning—we went to Canary Hill. He first wanted his favourite walk through the trees, but I hurried him along the climbing road which now stretched brown and dusty since it was winter, and the trees on either side were also covered in reddish-brown dust. Apart from a small car that groaned as it drove up, all was quiet. We hadn't gone more than a few hundred yards or so when he stopped and asked abruptly if we could turn back because he wasn't enjoying the walk at all with all that dust and noise, the latter of course no more than a purely inoffensive chugging of that humble car. This was gross over-reaction, but I could understand that the whole affair was based entirely on one's point of view. Having nothing more to say, I went back with him. The thing was that somehow Canary Hill wasn't quite the same to me after this little episode and I didn't really like him for it.

Arvind's Hour

'How long has it been since we last saw each other?' asked Arvind. I said it had been twenty years or so and we looked at each other with the kind of surprise that is generally the reaction when two people going their separate ways meet up unexpectedly.

Arvind did not live in Hazaribagh. He was from a town in a neighbouring district and went to school there. I would meet him when he travelled to Hazaribagh for a few days each winter. The reason for his visits was one of Hazaribagh's main sports attractions, the badminton competition in which clubs from the town as well from other places like Ranchi and Giridih took part. Arvind, passionate about the game, never missed a season. And I often found myself sitting beside him on cold winter evenings when the matches were played, lights blazing on the court, the air resonating with the 'ping-ping' staccato of the shuttlecock going back and forth and the intermittent clapping from the crowd.

Talking to Arvind, I gathered that in the upside and downside of his life, the downside was winning. The basics of course were alright. As the only son of loving parents (the other sibling, a married sister, lived away) his life at home was happy, and his father made a living as a contractor.

Things were good except for the one bane of Arvind's life. A boy in his class, son of a well-to-do trader, made his life an absolute trial. The father was a man of influence and this boy took full advantage. Arvind's tormentor, Hiru, seemed to have one consistent purpose and this was to subject Arvind to unending tricks which never failed to get him in trouble. Hiru's single-minded appetite for making Arvind's life difficult was inexhaustible, and it took on a whole variety of craftiness. He snitched on Arvind to the teachers. He let the air out of his cycle tyres. He cut out pages from his textbooks. He did all this with a cleverness that put him beyond suspicion.

But Hiru's specialty was sending out false summons, and he had perfected this art. He sent messages to Arvind through other boys or the school durwan. One day the message was that Arvind was wanted in the headmaster's room. The headmaster was much feared and it terrified Arvind since he had no idea why he had been called—which he hadn't been really. Another time the message was that Arvind's father was badly sick, at a place far from home. Arvind's mother was in a state, when he told her. When Arvind got to his father, panting and huffing in the summer heat, he realized the hoax. Once Arvind got a peremptory summons from Hiru's father who for some reason was apparently annoyed with him. Hiru's father was a powerful man in the community and it didn't do to keep him waiting. This was another ruse, and every time poor Arvind came away stung by embarrassment.

The beauty of Hiru's ploys was he never repeated them beyond once or twice a month. When he did, the carriers of the message were unknowing of the ploy and so gave the messages to Arvind in all innocence. Sometimes the hoax was in reverse. One day Hiru came up to Arvind to tell him his class teacher was waiting for him; he was unhappy with Arvind's homework. Knowing this to be another trick, Arvind avoided the trap. The problem, however, was that the class teacher was in fact waiting for him and, furious at the insubordination, complained to Arvind's father in no uncertain terms. Each time a message came, Arvind was caught in a flurry of doubt. What if the message was true? So he went along, fearing all the while that this was another bogus message. The hapless Arvind had become the butt of ridicule, and nobody shared his plight, not his classmates, not his teachers, and what was more painful, not even his father. He saw this all as a harmless prank, not seeing the mortification his son was going through. So Arvind decided to get even, but he wasn't anywhere as devious as Hiru who could easily see through his fumbling attempts. The hostile mood thus went up several notches, and their encounters became bitter, both of them trading insults and accusations. Both boys were linked by an implacable dislike and it stayed throughout their years in school.

My chance meeting with Arvind so many years later at a busy intersection in Kolkata brought back those memories. We sat for a long time over coffee and caught up with each other. I told him I was working in the corporate sector, but I was more interested in what

Arvind had been up to all these years. In the quiet of a corner table Arvind and I regarded each other, uncertain about how to renew the links from so long ago. Watching him I saw the change from a gangly, awkward lad to the self-assured young man who sat in front of me. He told me he had joined the police department after school, working his way up to inspector. His job meant frequent transfers which he didn't mind since there were just the two of them—he and his wife of five years. He was now in charge of a police station in a small Chhotanagpur town.

He wasn't at all put out when we went back to the days of his harassment. In fact Arvind took it with remarkable poise. 'It has long ceased to bother me. Schoolboy friendships last, but not schoolboy enmities,' he told me calmly. Did he keep track of Hiru? He did, 'And he's making lots of money. I haven't run into him for a long time, but really I don't bear him a grudge anymore. His father died and he's now running the business.' Arvind had either forgiven Hiru or dismissed him from his mind and I said I was glad. Awkwardly, Arvind looked at me for a moment, 'That's right and let me tell you about the time I actually met him a couple of years ago…' And I'm putting it down in his words as best as I remember them:

A lazy summer day, nothing was happening. I was in charge of our little thana (police station). For a couple of hours I was in town when I saw a bus pull up at the stand and a man got out with the others. It was none other than Hiru. He looked much the same, maybe a little heavier and obviously here on business. It was a surprise and without any conscious thought I found myself checking up on where he was staying; it was in a house not far away. I got back to the thana but unaccountably the sight of him brought back my old resentment. I was surprised at myself because the whole thing didn't matter any longer, but I couldn't help myself.

Later in the afternoon, two constables from the thana knocked on Hiru's door. Hiru opened the door and his jaw dropped when he saw them. They asked him to identify himself. He did and they told him he must come with them to the thana. Why was he wanted? Hiru asked nervously. The constables exchanged glances but said nothing. He asked again, getting more and more nervous. 'You are wanted at the thana' was all they told him. They got him in the jeep and drove towards the thana. By now Hiru was totally unnerved and his mind was in a whirl of questions and the likely consequences that he was sure were going to be awful. Why had they come for him? What had he done? The way he did business was certainly not always above board. Were they on to him? If they were, how much did they know? Why didn't they call for him in his hometown? Why had they waited? Hiru couldn't guess how he was being implicated but he knew that the fact he had been summoned by the police was bad enough for his business, for his standing, and for his family. Whatever it was, he thought desperately, he was in deep trouble.

They reached the thana, Hiru a bundle of nerves and

the stony silence of the constables didn't help. They pointed to a chair and brusquely asked him to sit and wait for 'saab' who was on his way. So Hiru waited and sweated in rising apprehension. 'Saab' was evidently taking his time. The longer he waited, the worse it got and by now fear had set in. Petrified of what was in store for him, he did something that was rare—he started praying to Lord Ganesh.

About an hour later 'saab' arrived. Hiru was called in to see him. He entered, full of foreboding, real fear on his face. Then he saw and recognized me at once. In his confusion, words failed him. Obviously, he hadn't kept up to date on me and didn't know that I was now a policeman. He stood there and gawked. 'Good to see you after such a long time, Hiru,' I said. 'I saw you getting off the bus and thought it would be nice to have a chat. Let's have some chai while we talk. And why are you looking worried? Is something wrong?' By then Hiru was a near wreck.

This was a neat trick, I told Arvind; neater than anything Hiru had ever played on him. But I couldn't help feeling sorry for Hiru; did he really, after all these years deserve the punishment and the tension Arvind's little game had put him through? 'Small price to pay,' Arvind told me with a grin.

STRANGE MEETINGS

Bholu's Friend

Sunlight played on the grey-brown coat of the fox as he lay on the grass in our mango grove. Something was wrong, and I immediately saw what it was. His left foreleg was at an odd angle, the ankle was swollen, the festering wound infected, and the tip of his left ear was missing. I guessed he had got into a bad scuffle with another fox, or a stray dog. He was frightened when I came near, and tried to get up and run but the pain was too much to take and he fell back, chest heaving.

This sad little scene was entirely at odds with the ambience of the afternoon. It was spring and the winds across the fields and meadows were getting warmer. The trees were splendidly green. Giant silk-cotton trees with their black branches and blood-red flowers made a stunning contrast against the vivid blue of the sky. Tall shoots from the sisal plants ended with circles of creamy white flowers around their tip. The new bark of the eucalyptus was stark white in the sun. The air was heavy with the smell of mango and mahua blossoms, and the incessant call of the koel came piercing sweet.

But the pain of this suffering animal took the joyous mood away.

Our gardener and I tried to pick him up, and he cowered in fear. Finally we managed to take him to the clinic where they patched up and dressed the wound, and gave him antibiotics. Luckily, there were no broken bones. We brought our fox home. Older than a cub, but not fully grown, he was certainly handsome with his rich coat and bushy tail. We settled him in our woodshed in the courtyard, and for the next two days he lay quietly, eating very little, but letting us change his dressing. Whenever we came to him with a new dressing, he would hold out his bandaged leg, as if to show how hurt he was.

After a week or so, his injuries had healed and the pain virtually gone. He spent most of the day exploring the nooks and corners of the courtyard. He was remarkably playful and frolicsome, chasing squirrels, and trying to frighten the sparrows. By now, his appetite had increased, and his favourites were bread soaked in milk, chicken pieces mixed in rice, and to our great amusement, lassi. He loved his lassi light and sweet.

The more he became used to people the more trusting he grew, and came to us without shyness or suspicion. Our gardener fondly named him Bholu, after his guileless nature, and the joke around the house was that Bholu, lacking cunning, must be an embarrassment to the cannier members of his species. This did not bother Bholu in the slightest. One day, I spoke to him teasingly about how gullible he was. Bholu looked up at me all the while, and when I paused, he lay down and was promptly asleep. There were other special moments. One afternoon I was sitting by the front steps. It was quiet, the only sound was the rustle of the wind as it stirred the leaves. Bholu appeared on the lawn. When I called out to him, he came, snuggled up to me, rested his chin on my knees and stayed quite still. It was an entrancing moment. I sat there unmoving; after a while Bholu stretched himself and trotted away.

Spring gave way to summer. Bholu spent his time in the garden, and in the fields and the terrain beyond it. Most days I saw him lying in the shadows of our mango grove, his favourite resting place. When it rained, particularly in the monsoon, he would cry out to be let in through the courtyard door to his woodshed shelter. He had a special cry for it, a kind of a coaxing purr which was his plea for shelter from the rain. His other call was at sundown—not the familiar raucous fox call. It was a long, trailing call, achingly sad and haunting, and we loved it.

It was more than six months since Bholu had come into our lives, and by now he was nearing adulthood. His gait was more confident, he went about the grounds with an easy assurance, frequently venturing beyond the house. By early autumn he was gone for three or four days at a time, but before we began to worry, he was back. I also realized something else, that when away for days he was clearly becoming capable of hunting for food—rabbit, partridge, quail. Because when he returned, he looked none the worse for wear.

One beautiful autumn evening, the sun was going down, its dying rays catching the fields and our garden. In the twilight silence, I waited for Bholu's call. It did not come that day, and not for days after that. Frantic with anxiety, we called for him endlessly, and searched for him in the fields and forest trails, but there was no sign of him. Our days alternated between hope and worry.

It was now more than three weeks since Bholu had disappeared, and I knew suddenly that he was not going to come back. The pain was in not knowing where he was, or how he was, or if something had happened to him.

One day, a friend and I were cycling towards the forest reserve which started about five miles from our home. It was well before noon, and we were going down the road that skirted the forest. Thirsty, we stopped to drink water from our bottles. Quite suddenly, we saw a fox and his mate crossing the road and about to enter the edge of the forest. They brought back memories of Bholu in a rush. To my utter astonishment, it was Bholu, unmistakable in his nicked ear, with his companion. The two of them were walking side by side in close togetherness. In my relief I called to him in a voice that did not sound like my own. Bholu froze, turned and looked at us. 'Bholu,' I called again softly. He came up to me, and with indefinable tenderness purred deep in his throat. We stayed like that for no more than a minute. Then he was gone, and he and his mate disappeared in the welcoming depths of the sal forest.

I felt at peace then, now that he was in his own world, and starting his life with his mate. But the days of companionable silence that were ours, my joy at his playfulness, of watching him doze contentedly in the shade of our mango grove, his plaintive cry as evening shadows deepened in our garden—these had passed into memory.

Playtime's End

The odd thing about the green bee-eater was that it spent long hours on the branches of the sal tree at a corner of our house even though its nest wasn't there. I first noticed it sometime in September when the monsoon was on its way out. This was a season when bee-eaters were more active, catching bees and insects which were plentiful after the rains. I saw this one flying from tree to tree, its emerald green plumage vivid in the afternoon sunlight. But the sal tree was not its home and it always flew away in the evening. I often wondered about the bee eater. Did it have a companion? Where did it fly away to in the evenings? Where was its nest, if it had one? Why was it always alone on the sal branch? It came always in the afternoon, staying till the sun went down.

And then I found a clue. The grass beneath our sal tree was the favourite resting place for a stray tomcat. He was large, with a thick bushy tail, rust-brown coat, and a face which carried the impression that he was perpetually sleepy. He would lie dozing peacefully, now and then opening one eye at the sound of approaching feet. And one day I saw him and the bee-eater at play. The cat lay curled up, eyes closed and the bee-eater flew down, fluttered over the cat and pecked at his tail or the back of his head. The cat waited for this move, twisted round to grab at the bee-eater, which in its turn circled round and the whole game began again. This was a show on most afternoons and I made a point of being there as often as I could, and always on Saturdays and Sundays. At sundown the game would be over, to begin again the next afternoon. No one could tell how the cat and the bird became playmates, but watching the bee-eater's playful mischief and the cat's mock aggression as they played happily was a delightful experience. Sometimes when the cat did not show up, the bee-eater sat waiting quietly on the branch before flying away at sundown.

One morning I found my mother standing by the roadside in front of our house and she was crying out in distress. The cat had been run over by a passing car and its poor broken body lay in a large stain of dried blood; he must have died the night before. We were desolated and I couldn't bring myself to go near the place where the cat used to lie sleeping, at peace with himself. We buried it in a quiet corner behind the house.

I was not ready for what I saw afterwards. In the late afternoon, the bee-eater flew around our sal tree, skimming low toward the ground where the cat rested, impatient for their game to begin. It came for days, giving its characteristic 'Kree, kree' call and searching despairingly for its playmate. It must have known somehow that its friend wasn't coming back, as though it also knew that you couldn't love anything too much in this world. Playtime was over at last and it flew away, never to return. Our sal tree and the little patch of grass were never the same anymore. In leaving, the bee-eater carried its loss with it, and left me with my own.

Bahadur's Puzzle

The field beyond our eastern boundary wall ran for about a thousand yards, broke into little folds (what we called 'khoai') and then dipped to a little stream. This was where the wild creatures came to drink at sunset. In the summer months, you could see them almost every day, but not as frequently during autumn and winter.

I loved watching them from behind a thick cluster of lantana bushes at the edge of the field. Sometimes I saw a group of quail or partridge, sometimes a fox or two, an occasional jungle cat or if I was lucky, a solitary deer, its ears perked for trouble. In the summer the stream was a trickle. But in the monsoon, swollen with rain, it became an angry torrent. The sound of its rushing waters was a constant background through the days and nights. During early autumn, the stream was still turbulent, quietening down with the coming of winter.

On an early September afternoon, I lay in wait by my hiding place. Hours passed, but nothing appeared by the stream side, not even a squirrel. After a futile wait, I got up to go home. The day was ending and the sun's last rays grazed the fields, the dips and hollows already in shadow. Far away, darkness touched the hills, turning them almost indistinguishable and featureless. A flock of herons flew silently by and there was an extraordinary stillness in the air. Standing there alone, I was aware of a presence, and before I knew what it was, it was right there in front of me, no more than twenty feet away. It was a full-grown wolf; curiously, and this was the strangest thing, I felt more surprise than fear. The wolf made no threatening move, and regarded me steadily, its golden yellow eyes full of intelligence. In the near darkness, the wolf, regal and proud, and I, by now terribly afraid and uncertain looked at each other in a kind of tableau. It could have been no more than a few seconds, and then the wolf snorted dismissively and was gone. For days afterwards, I wished I could see it one more time, but it never appeared.

The terrain behind our house was one of my favourite walks across fields and thickets till I came to Canary Hill. This was a wonderfully wooded country and it was a pleasure to walk in the shadows of sal and tamarind trees. I remember it was sometime in October that I was hiking home cross-country from Canary Hill. It was going to be dusk soon, and I was about to clear the woodland to open country on my way home when I knew suddenly that I was in desperate trouble. Approaching me was an adult hyena. I saw at once the threat of its lean, hard body, its vicious eyes and the way he thrust its long neck forward as he came towards me.

Hyenas are known to be group scavengers, and as far as I knew had little truck with adult humans, but clearly this one—a rogue hyena?—was an exception and up to no good. It paused, darted at me, then backed off and repeated the movement from another angle, testing me. I stood motionless, in a state of real fear. Two things happened then. From the rim of a depression in the ground close by, something emerged and the hyena, sensing the intrusion, turned towards it. It was a wolf. Was it the wolf that I had come across earlier? Was it another? I could not tell, conscious only of my fear.

What followed was totally unexpected. Without any kind of warning, the wolf went straight for the hyena. In a moment it had the hyena on the ground, giving it a mauling. The sounds were distinctive: the wolf growling savagely all the while and the hyena screeching in panic. The hyena wasn't fighting back, all it was trying to do was twist away which it was finally able to do. It ran, its body showing ugly gashes. The wolf did not chase it. Ignoring me completely, it loped back the way it came.

For days I tried unsuccessfully to make sense of what had happened. First, what perhaps protected me initially was that I had kept still, and the hyena may have been uncertain about how I would react. But the actual puzzle was the wolf. Wolves are hunters, so why should this one have attacked the hyena which clearly was not its prey? On the other hand, wolves are not generally friendly towards people, so what could then explain its action that saved me that day? Or did it have cubs close by and was defending its territory? Then again, an open terrain was no place for a wolf with cubs to protect. In any case, I thought the wolf was a hero, and in my mind, I gratefully named it Bahadur.

One evening late in October, I was in our front garden. In the closing darkness, I felt something was moving across our gate. I unconsciously visualized Bahadur, my wolf and saviour. I hurried outside to check. All was silent, and I could see nothing. Only the dim bulk of the surrounding trees. Somewhere from a distance an owl hooted mournfully, a drongo swooped low and disappeared into the darkness, a night heron glided by, ghostlike and noiseless, a sudden breeze stirred the leaves, but there was no sign of anything else. No Bahadur either. I walked back to the house, sad in knowing that I would never see it again.

Story of Fish

Past the sisal fields in front of our house, the tree-lined road ran for about a mile and then curved past the Hazaribagh lake. The lake was long and wide, its waters surrounded by trees and some bungalows of government officers. The place was nearly always quiet, except for some occasional strollers.

Dhanua, a gardener in one of the houses close to the lake, was my companion during some afternoons. We walked along the banks of the lake in silence, watching the play of light and clouds on the water, and loving the stillness. It was after our third or fourth walk together that Dhanua told me about the fish in the lake. I knew that the lake was full of fish, since there was a strict ban on fishing. Dhanua though was talking of a particular fish, one he said was a veteran of these waters. He had seen this fish many times, and said he would show it to me when we came there next.

In his mid-fifties, Dhanua looked much older. His skin had the texture of old, wrinkled leather, and his hands reminded me of the gnarled, ancient tree in his garden. But his eyes were kind. He shared with me many secrets of the landscape and wildlife: how the call of a grouse was different when it was afraid of a predator, how to tell that a dried teak leaf was in fact a rabbit's ear when it was in camouflage, how to tell whether a cornered snake was going to lunge or slither away, how to predict oncoming rain on a clear day. Which was why I asked him about the fish: when he first saw it, and what was so special about it. I realized immediately that this was a mistake. Dhanua, like many village folk felt time differently, more as a matter-of-fact presence than something to race against. This, as I understood gradually, was understandable, because in his unchanging occupation in a largely unchanging landscape, time was unobtrusive, with no real need for measuring. So he informed me that he first saw the fish two or three years ago. Could he be more specific? Yes, he said, it was when he had jukam. And when was this? '*Teen ya char barsat pehle*,' he clarified. I gave up, but Dhanua did promise to show me the fish.

One afternoon Dhanua and I walked to the lake. It was a day typical of an early Hazaribagh summer. The ground was a patchwork of colour: the vivid purple of ripened blackberries as they fell to the ground from the branches and the varied reds of shimul and krishnachura as they lay randomly scattered. The air was heavy with the overpowering smell of mahua as birds pecked on their oversweet pulp and of mangoes ripening in the sun.

Dhanua took me to a spot by the lake, and we settled down on the ground to wait. Dhanua warned me that I must be patient, and absolutely silent, and we sat quietly. We waited in the still and warm afternoon, no breeze, the leaves on trees hanging limp, the water smooth as glass. After some time I whispered, 'No luck yet.' Dhanua didn't bother to reply, but after another fifteen minutes or so, asked whether I expected the fish to appear with all my 'chatter'. Minutes passed, and I must have lost attention after a while because Dhanua was clutching my knee in signal.

Something was moving in the water. It looked at first like a gliding shadow and then I saw it more clearly. It was a huge carp (or katla, as we knew it). It seemed to me to be all of four feet in length. The fish was weaving in and out between the reeds in lazy, supple movement close to where we sat, its body dappled by sunlight through the clear water. I had never before seen a fish in its natural environment, and I was transfixed. The ordinariness of fish disappeared in an instant, and this one looked exotic and mysterious, from an almost unknown place beneath the waters.

The carp swam about lazily—coming close to where we were, moving away. Dhanua took out some pieces of bread from his bag and dropped them in the lake. Nothing happened for a few moments, and then the carp swam in close and delicately picked up the pieces one by one. The show wasn't over yet. In a leap, it cleared the water in a graceful arc, its dark-grey body catching the sun, caught a crumb in mid-air, and dived back into the water. Then it swam away.

I made Dhanua promise he would be with me at the lake as often as possible. Dhanua kept his promise, and we would go there at least once a week and wait for our carp. Sometimes it came, and I was saddened when sometimes it didn't. Once I asked Dhanua if others had seen the fish. He said no, because he doubted if anyone knew of this fish, and in any case people didn't have the patience to wait for it. Did Dhanua think that the fish recognized us? He looked at me with an expression that said I was being stupid. But I wasn't sure, and imagined fondly that perhaps we were something more than a food source to the fish, and that it came to us in trust. I didn't dwell much on it, and was simply happy that the fish came to us unbidden at the lakeside.

One morning, the government surprisingly allowed a day of fishing. I had no idea if this was a culling exercise. My father, being fond of fish, asked me to get one. When I reached the lake, the nets were already cast. It was quite a spectacle, and a small crowd had gathered to see the varieties of fish that were being netted. When the next catch was hauled in there was a gasp from onlookers. Dwarfing the rest of the catch was a fish, and shockingly, it was our carp. Everyone was amazed at its size. Our carp was lying on the grass, its enormous body without life. In death it lay in a kind of sad majesty and looked even larger than I thought it was. I wasn't seeing a dead fish, I was seeing the days we spent watching its wondrous grace as it glided contentedly in its own waters, and its unsuspecting approach as we waited for it to come.

I felt pain then as I had hardly known before and a lump rose in my throat. I turned away, grieving the loss of something that had brought Dhanua and me so much joy. I returned home in the hot summer sun, the memory of our beautiful fish in my mind. It stayed with me all day long, and into the night, and it was there as the first light of daybreak came in through my window.

His First Tipple

A hot afternoon in early April. The heat hung heavy and all were indoors, waiting for evening. The road in front of the gate was empty. I don't remember why Mali our gardener ventured out, and when he came back, he made me go out with him towards a mahua tree a little way from our gate.

On the ground beneath the tree was a baby bear; as I recall it was a sloth bear. It was a male cub, hopelessly woozy from eating the mahua flowers that fell from the branches. Summer months in Hazaribagh were fragrant with mahua, a huge favourite with villagers who brewed it into potent toddy. And bears loved mahua. If in summer one went to the jungle, or a lonely stretch of road with a mahua tree beside it, they were likely to come across bear footmarks where the flowers had dropped.

This bear cub had of course strayed from his mother and was in no position to help himself. He was on his back, and tried unsuccessfully to get up on his legs but rolled over each time, like a plump little bundle. After a few attempts, he lay still, staring, catching his breath before trying again. It really was comical and I was laughing till Mali told me that we needed to get the bear inside the house before he got into trouble and wait till his mother came for him. Mali was carrying his net. When we picked the bear up, he was totally unresisting and uncomprehending because all that mahua had gone to his head.

So he stayed the night in our woodshed by the courtyard. He refused food and went to sleep. He made no noise during the night, and slept soundly. In the morning he was scratching on the woodshed door and when we brought him out he looked alert and in his senses, blinking in the summer sunlight.

Continually turning his head this way and that, he looked for his mother and this was sad to watch. He didn't want any food but drank some water and gave soft, purring cries. Mali said that the mother bear was sure to come looking for her cub sooner or later and we waited, the cub never ceasing his plaintive calls. Late afternoon, Mali called us in excitement. Well beyond our gate, beyond the lone mahua tree on the other side of the road and on the edge of a cluster of sal trees, the mother bear was waiting. Bears are generally silent animals, crying out only when angry or agitated. The mother stood unmoving, but her anxiety was plain from her deep, 'huff-huff' calls. How she came near the spot where we found the cub was a mystery, but there she was.

Mali gently led the cub from our courtyard to the front gate. We kept our distance, unsure how the mother would react if she felt our presence was a danger. We led him out of the gate, and he saw his mother at once and broke off into a waddling run. The mother waited. The cub came up to her and began to nuzzle her in relief and she nuzzled back. She then gently nudged him ahead of her and together they disappeared into the sal trees. Smiling, my mother observed that the cub had started somewhat early on his career as a tippler.

Oddity Encounters

At first it looked like a length of rope on the ground, a few yards from where I looked out from the edge of our back garden. It was an afternoon well into autumn and the thing in front that contrasted clearly against the grass still green from the rains, suddenly showed a ripple of movement. It was a full-grown snake, although I don't remember what variety it was. In sinuous grace it glided, its grey-brown body clear in the sunlight, and it was making for the hollow in the ground in front of it. It moved swiftly, then slowed, stopped, waited and moved forward again in typical predator fashion.

I didn't see its prey but the calls from the bushes in the hollow meant it was a clutch of partridges calling in fear. The snake was sure of its prey and with deliberate slowness it inched closer to the bushes till it came to a stop, ready now to strike. Then it happened. Out of the undergrowth flew the mother—or father—partridge.

Partridges spend most of their life evading predators, their only defence being their uncanny instinct that warns them of danger. They are totally unequipped for aggression. This partridge defied its timid image. It was angry and what came out of the bush was not a frightened bird flying away, but flying directly at the snake. It came screeching, a ball of fury, desperate to protect its chicks hidden in the hollow, and the contest began. The snake waited for the partridge to come within range, its body tensed in a characteristic 'S'. The partridge came in low, the snake reared up and struck. It missed and the snake immediately coiled into another 'S', waiting to make the next strike. The partridge, for all its plumpness, proved to be remarkably agile. It fluttered high, swooped down and pecked wickedly at the snake's head. It too missed, but not entirely. It struck the snake on the neck before moving away. The snake turned to face the partridge, now coming from another direction and used its only attack mode—the deadly upthrust of its neck and fangs. This went on for a while but by now it was clear that the battle was not really between unequals, and if anything, it was the partridge that held the edge. It confused the snake with the rapid flutter of its wings and the unpredictable approach of attack from above. Soon the snake was losing its reflex and speed. Its upward darts were slower, while the partridge kept out of harm's way, pecking repeatedly and pecking hard. The snake began to run out of ideas, its head and body showing cruel cuts bright with blood. Futilely it tried again, rearing up to get at the partridge, which kept continuously beyond range. As soon as the snake finished its strike, it was out of balance, slower now to get back to its coiled 'S' position, and the partridge came in fast for another blow. It didn't last for very long. The snake, now a mangled, bloody mess, had had enough and crawled away.

~

In the stillness of the summer afternoon, everything was quiet, except for the sound of a dove's call somewhere in the distance. The gully outside our garden's boundary wall was partly in shadow where the rabbit rested contentedly. In camouflage, it blended perfectly with the colour and texture of the terrain, and its excellent hearing gave it immediate danger signals. But the rabbit was fractionally late in detecting the fox as it approached slowly. The fox then broke into a rush and, knowing it was in trouble, the rabbit took off in a long, bounding run. The problem was that in the open ground there was no cover for the rabbit. Although the rabbit had the speed characteristic of its species, the chase was getting shorter with the fox closing in, and it was only a matter of minutes before the fox grabbed its lunch. The rabbit, knowing that its camouflage was blown and its speed no longer an advantage, decided to stand its ground and defend itself. That was exactly what the fox was waiting for, because rushing in for the final pounce was now easy. But the fox took its time. He circled round the rabbit, aiming to attack from the side, but in this he was frustrated. As soon as it got close, the rabbit turned its back on it, adopting its last defence which was kicking out with its strong hind legs. The fox avoided this easily and then renewed its lunge. This stalemate of course was bound to end and there was no doubt that the fox would get his lunch in the end.

Except that the end was unexpected. So far the fox had sidestepped the rabbit's kicks with no trouble, but at this stage of the proceedings he became slightly careless and that finished the contest. A kick from the rabbit got home and it caught the fox flush on the nose. It was pure luck. The fox rolled over at the blow and was more surprised than hurt, unbelieving this was happening to it and wanting no further part in the exchange. Both ran—the rabbit for its life and the fox in embarrassed retreat.

Two Trees

Not far from the edge of our garden wall stood a pair of gulmohar trees, and as far as I knew, their brilliantly vivid yellow flowers belonged to the laburnum family, popularly known as 'yellow gulmohar'. The slope and fields stretching away from there came to thick lines of trees—mango, sal, shegun, eucalyptus, each growing in clusters.

Our two gulmohars were on a totally opposite setting. On open ground, they stood by themselves close to each other, no other trees nearby. Gulmohars standing in groups were common enough, but these two, lonely in that open field, looked as though they had grown there by accident—remote and away from their kind and in a landscape alien to them. These trees were my neighbours ever since I began to live in Hazaribagh, and it was a delight seeing them change according to the rhythms of seasons. In winter months they were bare, their branches skeletal to the sky, very few leaves on them. Fresh parrot-green leaves covered the branches from February and then appeared countless dark brown buds. By the time summer came around, they blossomed in wild profusion, the flowers coming out in waves of yellow. And ceaselessly, from morning to noon to night, the flowers overloading the branches drifted down to make a brilliant carpet on the ground. Summer was their time of glory, and by July their colours faded away, the trees standing quietly as if in a state of rest after the untiring blossoming during spring and summer.

It was late spring when one of the gulmohars had something else to offer. One afternoon a pair of woodpeckers was flying in and out of a hollow in the tree, about fifteen feet above the ground. All day I could hear the tapping the pair made to each other, which was their way of communicating as they went about building their nest.

Finally, I could tell that it was ready because the woodpeckers were no longer carrying leaves or twigs to line their nest. About three weeks later I found my mother standing under the tree, pointing out to me the hollow above her and I gazed in wonder. The eggs had hatched. Three tiny heads peeked out, beaks open, and the woodpeckers were flying back and forth, feeding the chicks worms, seeds and such. The chicks had obviously hatched more than a week before because their eyes were not shut and feathers had begun to appear.

The next few weeks were a time of innocent surprise as I watched the chicks progress from their fledgling state. First they came out and perched on the branch close to their nest. Later with increasing courage, they hopped about experimentally from branch to branch, watched over by either parent. Finally about a month later, they took their first faltering flights away from the tree, helped along by the parents. Once, one of the chicks fell to the ground. Frightened, it lay there completely still, its wings bunched tight. Mother- or father-woodpecker flew down, and patiently nudged it with its beak till it flew again. Around this time they learnt to forage for food, and I was fascinated by their transformation. Throughout their journey into adulthood, the gulmohar was the only home they knew.

It always struck me as curious, the way in which we tend to define things around us by events and circumstances surrounding them, giving them a dimension which is almost human. The gulmohar was a tree with all the attributes of its kind, and like countless other trees it also had a bird nest. It was only a tree. But the presence of this particular gulmohar seemed to be something more. It was as though the tree consciously provided the lasting comfort of shelter and shade as the woodpecker family played out in miniature the endless cycle of birth and rearing.

Suddenly one day, short of a month since the hatching, the entire woodpecker family—father, mother and chicks flew away and did not return. It was just that the chicks had reached maturity and were now independent to go their own way. I missed them badly, but my thoughts were with the tree. It stood as it always had, tall and gorgeous, but in my eyes it looked sad and deserted, like an empty house where nothing lived anymore.

It was now early autumn, monsoon was on the way out, but untypically for September a heavy squall came in the evening, bringing with it rain and a fierce windstorm. From evening till before daybreak the wind raged in one of the worst storms I had ever seen. In the morning all was quiet. The garden was a shambles, and the storm had felled the two gulmohars outside our house. The smaller of the two was completely uprooted. The other, which was the woodpeckers' home, was snapped at the trunk. Both trees, their branches lying unnaturally on the ground, looked like corpses.

Gloom descended on the house, and it was wrenching to see the space where the trees once stood, and where only the trunk of one showed, black and jagged on the grass. Autumn came and went, and winter, and soon it would be spring. On a day towards the end of February, something miraculous happened. From the tree stump, which earlier looked lifeless, wasted and barren, tender green shoots appeared. More emerged in the weeks that followed, and soon they were turning into branches, growing sturdier and sturdier. The renewal took my breath away. Our gulmohar had come back to life, indestructible after all.

Weather Report

'Thank God it has stopped raining,' said my fellow passenger in the departure lounge as we waited for our flight from Chennai to Kolkata. On his way back from his first trip to Chennai, he told me he was puzzled that at that time of year—November—the city was getting heavy rains every day. 'In November, imagine!' He was taken aback by such 'unseasonal' rains. Quite obviously he was unaware that Chennai, like other places in South India, experienced the 'return' monsoon.

Hearing him talk of 'unseasonal' November rains brought back images from my long-ago boyhood memories of Hazaribagh. The predictability of changing seasons meant we knew how each season came with its tone and texture. In all my years in Hazaribagh though, there were three scenes that I remember that qualified as 'unseasonal'. They were absolutely special in their unusualness and I'm putting them down although they are by no means stories. Way beyond unseasonal, actually they were freakish aberrations that I had not seen before or since.

With the winter approaching in late October, the weather was sharp and clear. The skies were empty barring some scattered white clouds which weren't rain clouds at all. October through February were generally dry, cold months that were defined by dew, mist and early sundown. There was a chill to that October evening as I cycled home from school after my chemistry practical. In the late moon that was rising, the sky looked bare but a while later the look of the sky changed. It was now under an almost transparent cloud cover, like a thin sheet of gauze, pale moonlight filtering through. Then it started to rain. It wasn't even a light drizzle. It was close to impalpable, coming down in thin slanting lines, silver in the indistinct moonlight. The whole scene was startlingly beautiful; the surrounding countryside was silent. Fields, trees and hedges on either side of the road slept under the faint glimmer of the moon. Lines of rain, an unearthly white, fell without a sound. Alone on that road, I got off my bicycle. I wasn't pedalling, I was walking it slowly, taking in the wonder of it all. The rain that came from a sky that had no clouds to speak of, the moon only dimly visible, created a mood that was mysterious and breathtaking; you couldn't pin it down to any specific time of year and I felt I was lucky to have been a part of it.

~

May, the hottest summer month. Mali, our gardener-cum-caretaker and I were the two people in our home, my parents away for a few days in Giridih with my sister's family. The night was hot and we took a walk in the garden before turning in. It was well after midnight when I woke up. There wasn't any noise, no disturbance of any kind but something definitely was happening outside. I went out to the courtyard and was wide-eyed.

In the hot summer night thin, winding wisps of cloud streamed down noiselessly. They weren't clouds really, they were as wraiths and as insubstantial. Ghost-like, almost spectral, they floated at ground level, swirling across the courtyard and in and out of the rooms through windows that were open. Cloud wisps at ground level? In Hazaribagh, which didn't have the altitude for this kind of scenario? It was unreal, almost like a fantasy. Excitedly I called Mali who stood and gaped at the scene. In all his sixty years, he hadn't seen anything like what he was seeing now, he said, awe in his voice. Both of us stood, alone in that enchanted night as the strange scene played itself out around us.

~

A few miles away from our house and along the highway, a turn from the road broke off into undulating land which led to a little waterfall. Actually it was more a stream flowing over a few large boulders. The place was totally secluded, surrounded by sal trees. The only sounds were the soft lapping of water and sporadic bird calls. It was a place a friend and I went to often in the daytime.

One afternoon, when autumn was around the corner we cycled to our favourite place. We splashed about in the 'waterfall', which then was little more than a trickle and we walked the wooded terrain in the quiet of the afternoon before finally deciding to head homeward. The sun was still strong when we were about to return. But something in the landscape was no longer the same.

Dusk was well away, but low, heavy clouds had now taken over the sky from one end to the other, and everything was suddenly dark. Everything, except for where we were. The place we stood was bright in sunlight, but no more than thirty yards or so away, the ground and the trees were in near complete darkness. It was as though we were on an island that was sunlit but surrounded by nightfall. Far away from the highway on that lonely landscape, and in the utter quiet, the darkness looked sinister. And being at home seemed a far better prospect than this place where we were. We stood, bewildered and afraid at this bizarre scene. It didn't last beyond some minutes at the most and then the sun shone once more.

Light and darkness in a cloud-ridden landscape was nothing more than an ordinary phenomenon and yet this particular spot where we stood, one that was totally familiar and commonplace was now changed beyond recognition. We stood on the sunlit patch; the surrounding terrain suddenly dark and threatening, and the utter stillness in the air filled us with a menace of we knew not what. It was as though the trees and the rocks around us, dark and brooding, had taken on a strange malignity. It was as though a nameless danger would engulf us, and suddenly I shivered. Cycling back as fast as we could, my friend and I told each other that this was all fanciful nonsense, but the strange feeling of dread did not go away.

MENTORS AND MATES

Founder Father

In February 1951, a small group of Jesuit priests from Australia arrived in India. They were headed for Chhotanagpur. Among the six was John Moore, the founder and Rector-Principal of St Xavier's School which opened in Hazaribagh in 1952.

John Moore was then in his early thirties and quite suddenly he found himself with responsibilities that were both huge and complex. Besides organizing the school's infrastructure in all its details, there were other responsibilities he had to take up straightaway. These included completing formalities with the local administration, selecting capable teachers in Hazaribagh to support the Jesuit teaching faculty, creating the school's academic profile, sourcing textbooks, starting the school library. And most important, setting down the school's vision statement.

In those days when the school was being set up, there was another man—among many others—who worked closely with John Moore. He was Brother Nicholi Bilic. He went to Hazaribagh and worked closely with Father Moore. Lean and leathery, arms burly from years of outdoor work, Brother Bilic was responsible for executing the construction of the new building, dormitories, the main office, the infirmary and the dining hall. He built furniture, including desks, lockers, tables and chairs and we found the ringing sounds from his carpentry shop curiously comforting. A few years later Father Moore was joined by Father Kevin Grogan. Over the years Grogan became a legend at St Xavier's, Hazaribagh. And that's another story.

John Moore pioneered St Xavier's when it opened in January 1952 to a group of boarders and some day scholars. It was a small start, but John Moore was expanding the campus, and the number of boarders and day students began to increase. Parents from surrounding industrial towns were anxious that their boys study in a peaceful and congenial setting. The school's reputation grew quickly and parents from Calcutta, Delhi and other cities were soon sending their sons to Hazaribagh in large numbers, because of the respect and goodwill John Moore and his team now enjoyed. It became a matter of pleasure for parents to say that their sons were studying in 'Father Moore's school'. More and more Jesuits were coming from Australia and some names come rushing back to me: Cronin, Thwaites, Dullard, Jones, Doyle, Donnelly, Walsh, Slattery, Schockhaert, Mulhearn, Burns, Dwyer Lees, Keogh, Grogan. All were wonderful mentors and a real privilege to know.

Parents saw John Moore as one who went beyond the boundaries of administrator and educator. To them he wasn't only the rector. He showed the imagination required to run a school and accepted the need for discipline, but not at the expense of the spontaneous joys of boyhood. John Moore detested the idea of discipline for the sake of discipline; he often said it was acceptable when it was used to impart values, but when it became punitive it showed up the failings of the one who wielded it.

I first met Father Moore in July 1954 when he interviewed me for admission. What I saw was an unremarkable-looking man, but when he spoke to me and shared what he expected of me, I saw someone exceptional, someone to look up to. Through the months and years I grew to realize what an absolutely special person he was—serious, not stern; firm, not harsh; caring, not demonstrative. But his humour never failed him. I can picture him sharing his enjoyment of some schoolboy howlers. He would laugh at some uproarious answers that came from some answer papers. It was his own brand of laughter, a deep-throated, indrawn 'reverse' chuckle that lit up his face.

How did John Moore envision his school? He had a clear vision of how he saw St Xavier's. It would not be an institution that merely gave out degrees to students graduating. It would be a place for developing character and self-esteem. It would be about building values and respect for others. It would be about knowledge beyond the textbook. It would be a place where boys would be inspired by India's timeless legacy. This wasn't the luxury of soaring rhetoric. What John Moore was doing was setting down his simple conviction about how he saw St Xavier's as the medium of true education. This was his mission statement that inspired the school's teaching faculty.

One of the first things John Moore did when he set up St Xavier's was to straightaway reject the idea of social distinction. Boys came from backgrounds as disparate as you could imagine. They came from affluent and poor families, from different communities and religions, from different parts of India, though mainly from the east and north. But they did things together. Distinction was out. John Moore's interaction with parents was the stuff of school gossip. He had all the time to understand a boy's anxieties and never failed to work on allaying them.

He was irascible when some parents were overprotective and clinging, or demanded 'the best' for their boys. Could his son be given 'special' food, a parent asked once. John Moore said he could suggest a number of hotels, though not in Hazaribagh. Another parent complained that his son had been struck by another boy. John Moore asked the parent what it was that irked him more—was it that his son was hurt in a scuffle? Or was it that the boy who hit him belonged to a very poor family? The father was indignant, he had not sent his son to St Xavier's to be roughed up. In that case, John Moore said serenely, he was welcome to take his son away. Or he could let his son learn to hold his own in a fight. Another time, a boy's father said his wife was distressed that her son had not written in two weeks. John Moore patiently told the father that their son was finding his place in a boy's world and enjoying the experience. An oversight of delay meant nothing. If anything demanded his parents' concern, he would not fail to let him know, he said. It was both an assurance and a rebuke. But parents who sent their sons to Hazaribagh were satisfied parents, knowing that their sons were being well cared for. And he had a rather unusual way of removing grievances. There were two boys in our class who were for some reason intractably hostile towards each other. Counselling failed and John Moore ordered the two boys to share the same table during meals every day, and to attend the chemistry and physics practical together as a pair. Did this work? It did.

John Moore, Kevin Grogan and the other Jesuits who taught in Hazaribagh showed no missionary zeal. They were keen on education without dogma and helping boys to grow with a clear perception of values. John Moore insisted on a wide curriculum. He introduced Sanskrit, Latin and even French in the middle classes. When someone suggested that St Xavier's was special because it was an English-medium school, John Moore's irritation was immediate. 'You mean elitist,' he retorted. English as the medium of teaching had nothing whatsoever to do with exclusiveness; it was necessary for a wider field of knowledge.

It was in our senior classes that our interaction with John Moore—'boss' as we called him—became more serious and mature. Ethics was one of his subjects with us and he taught it without undertones or overtones of religious dogma. He talked to us about what humanism meant, how living it was central to our life. Without sentimentality, he talked about the value of empathy in what he saw as an increasingly impersonal world. He talked about life as a relational experience and a need for concern beyond oneself. He constantly urged us to help others in ways that we could and I remember some incidents. One of them was about Fr Grogan's red pony. It grazed happily in our fields, always placid and gentle and Grogan's Man Friday, a boy called Prema, was in charge of looking after him. Prema and the pony were inseparable, and a familiar sight was Prema feeding him, brushing his coat, and walking alongside when a small boy from a junior class would get on the pony, crying out in delight as it ambled on the grounds. Then one day the pony fell ill. He couldn't get up, lying down and looking doleful. Prema, distraught, ran to inform Fr Grogan who called a vet from Ranchi. It was a bad stomach ailment and the treatment started. The pony recovered completely in little more than a week, but Prema's anguish was something to see. Not a day went by during that time when boys did not spend time with Prema, cheering him up and telling him that his pony was going to be all right.

Then there was the incident of the young carpenter in Brother Bilic's workshop. He had cut his hand on a chisel. He was bleeding badly and Brother Bilic was in town buying supplies. The wound was more dramatic than serious. It was a flesh wound but the sight of blood was unnerving. Some senior boys ran to John Moore who said nothing but looked at the boys steadily, waiting for their response. This was enough. They rushed to the carpentry shop, dressed and bandaged the wound—although unskilfully—and took him to the hospital to be treated properly. The roll call of such incidents can go on and on.

'Life is much bigger than examinations and career,' he

said often. We owed it to ourselves and to our families to find fulfilment and success in our career, but always we must be masters of our career—it mustn't be the other way around. Life found meaning through concern for people, he reminded us and was fond of quoting Donne's lines 'No man is an island…' With a touch of humour, he ridiculed what he called the 'house, wife, car' syndrome many young people seemed to live by. You judged success not by how much you earned or how well liked you were, but by your integrity as a man.

John Moore was dismayed by what he saw as the mindless materialism finding its way into the lives of young people, calling it one of West's lasting contributions to India. He never tired of stressing the need to go back to India's cultural roots and the legacy of her wisdom, something he said was being fast forgotten. Was British colonialism responsible for this? John Moore would be quick to remind us that only a fool would deny the great work that so many Englishmen had done in India, for India and on India. But the ugly legacy of colonialism was visible always. Once he read out to us Macaulay's famous minutes on Indian education in which the great statesman had contemptuously disparaged the tradition of Indian learning. It wasn't about scholarship, John Moore said. It was about ignorance and the monumental Western arrogance of the time. If you were ignorant of your heritage, you mortgaged your character.

By the '60s, St Xavier's Hazaribagh had been established as one of India's finest schools and John

Moore was assigned to set up a new St Xavier's school in Bokaro Steel City. He brought to this school the same energy and vision that so characterized him.

John Moore's interaction with parents revealed his innermost beliefs on the purpose of education. Once, speaking to parents in Bokaro, he said, 'I do not think that when God asks us for an account of our stewardship, examination results will figure very prominently in that audit.' He saw education in its widest sense and as the basis for human consciousness. It was about opening up minds, about freedom from prejudice. It was about preparing for life, not merely preparing for a job. It was about knowledge rather than a set of skills. It was about individual responsibility, of a man's place in the scheme of things, not merely his own scheme of things. He spent his life on this conviction, something that he propagated tirelessly.

He was clear about the dangers of misapplying dogma to education. But he never wavered in the belief that the process of growing up integrated and whole must be based on spiritual and ethical values. By today's standards of scepticism, this could well be risible, but we knew he wouldn't have cared if it was.

This wonderful man died in Hazaribagh on 2 October 1988, seated in his armchair on his verandah. In death he looked completely peaceful, no sign of suffering or distress. It is said that the book by his side had a marker with the lines from Wordsworth: 'The best portions of a good man's life: his little, nameless acts of kindness and love.'

After passing my Senior Cambridge exams in 1962, I left for Calcutta for my undergraduate studies. I went to see Father Moore to say goodbye. In the coolness of his room on that warm summer day, we spent a long time sharing our memories of how the school grew, the things we read, the games we played, the races we ran and the inseparable part of our lives that St Xavier's had become. He spoke of the exciting times ahead for me: college, university and then entering the world of profession. He wished me the best of success, and said, 'Remember always that doing well in life and living a good life are not the same.' I left carrying with me his letter introducing me to Father Bonhome who was then the principal of St Xavier's College, Calcutta. As I was leaving Hazaribagh and about to enter the next phase of my life, I asked myself what I had learned from this simple but profoundly wise man. And I knew that in my earlier years all that he shared with us was only part understood. But they rang clearer and truer as the years passed.

My father died after a sudden illness which was why by the time I went to Calcutta, classes in St Xavier's College had already begun more than two weeks ago. Being the disciplinarian Fr Bonhome was, I feared he would make no room for lateness. Nervously I gave him Fr Moore's letter. He read it, looked up and said, 'Right, off you go to class. You can do the formalities tomorrow, I'll talk to Father Moore today. Another thing, you could not hope for a finer mentor.'

Aditi and the Mallard

One afternoon, recalling our school days in one of those drifting conversations, I asked Aditi Nath, my friend of more than fifty years, if he remembered the incident of the Mallard. Nodding, he gave a sheepish grin and the entire thing came back vividly.

I was already at St Xavier's school in Hazaribagh when Aditi Nath Sarkar from Calcutta joined our class, three years before our school leaving Senior Cambridge exams. Our school was all a boy could ask for. Run by Australian Jesuits, it stood among huge grounds, one of them skirted by a mango orchard and a screen of graceful eucalyptus trees. It had top-rate infrastructure for studies, sports and games and it had a splendid library. Unclouded by dogma, it had an open, transparent atmosphere that encouraged dialogue. Aditi settled straightaway into his new surroundings, and his infectious humour and the width of his interests were an instant hit with others.

One day, some months after Aditi came to St Xavier's, talk went that he was 'making something' in the school craft room. We found him working away on a model aircraft which he told us was a Mallard, after that variety of duck. His enthusiasm about what he was doing caught up with us and we eagerly followed the progress of his model in the making. The plywood was cut into wings, sanded down and finished. So were the fuselage and tailfin. The airscrew was a 'Taifun', a German model Aditi had managed to acquire. As the model began to take shape, our involvement began to grow.

Finally, the Mallard was ready. Its elegant, upswept dihedral wings resembled those ducks that flew long distances. The plane looked more like an experimental glider with an airscrew fitted on. Beautifully slender and painted in fancy blue and yellow, it was ready for flight. There was excitement as Aditi set about preparing for what we called 'the flight of the Mallard'. Aditi took his plane to one of our playgrounds—called the Top Oval—and we followed. He turned the airscrew but nothing happened. He tried again and then again, but no luck. Then all of a sudden, the propeller moved, shimmered and quickly became a blur. With a whine the Mallard lifted with perfect grace in a climbing turn. A little later it hit a tree and crashed. There was collective dismay, and what was a beautiful plane a few minutes ago was now a crumpled wreck, one wing and the body broken.

I couldn't tell who was more saddened—Aditi or us. He did not make much of it, but our disappointment was keen at the thought that the result of his long, painstaking work was not to last beyond a few minutes and some of us marked the day as the day Aditi's Mallard crashed. But had it really? Thinking back on it years later, it seemed to me that it wasn't so after all. Because for some of us that day it was more than the crash of a toy plane. In a way, the Mallard took us beyond the edge of what we knew, and into the sphere of curiosity. To me it showed once again that knowledge could be fun, something to be enjoyed. I remember that this tiny plane opened up my own interest—one that has lasted to this day—in aircraft.

And some days later Aditi was busy making a model of the Mustang P-51 of the US Air Force, one of the finest combat aircraft of the Second World War. The blueprint was all laid out in the craft room, but somehow Aditi did not finish the model, and it didn't get off the workbench. But even from its rudimentary profile, I could make out that were it to be finished, it would have looked wondrously graceful and I remember this further opened up my fascination with the beauty of aircraft. I had no idea that a weapon of war could look so beautiful and I was soon poring over books from our library and discovering the sleek profile of other immortal aircraft of the war years: Spitfire and Hurricane, Messerschmitt and Focke-Wulf, Lightning and Corsair, Zero and Nakajima.

Aditi Nath need not have looked sheepish at all when I asked him about his Mallard so many years later. Because in a few minutes of flight, it did much more than crash. It led me to the wonderful grace of flight and it caught the imagination.

Helping Hand

He was about my age, perhaps a year or two older, and when I first met him I wasn't sure if I liked him. Saroj was his name and he lived near Hazaribagh's town centre. He studied at the local day school, he said. His father, a widower of some years and an office clerk, was in a state of running financial predicament. But Saroj was another proposition and there was something worldly-wise about him that made me vaguely uneasy. He didn't seem to have a care in the world.

Later though, I sometimes found him fun to be with, and now and then I found myself in his company. With his expertise we explored the town—such and such eating place served the best samosas, he would say knowledgeably. Or he would take me to a particular store, which he said sold household things at a cheaper price to his friends. He had very good contacts with the town's main cycle-repair shop—all I had to do was mention his name for instant service, he assured me with typical nonchalance. He also tried to tempt me to the improprieties of a surreptitious drag or two on a cigarette, or going truant to catch a new film that was running in the local theatre. As it happened he wasn't successful simply because I couldn't stand cigarette smoke anyway; and skipping classes made no sense because I enjoyed my classes. In any case, there would be a big price to pay if the school found out what

I'd been up to. He was fun, as I said, but we were not friends.

One morning my mother sent me to town to make some purchases for the house and I came across Saroj. Curiously, he wasn't his usual breezy self and looked distraught. His father hadn't been able to clear the backlog on his school fees, which meant Saroj wasn't going to be allowed to sit for his final exams. He looked despairingly at me. I understood of course what this meant—he was about to lose one whole year unless his fees were paid. I didn't know what to say, and then, hesitating and embarrassed, he asked if I could lend him the money which as I recall was about a hundred rupees—a large amount in the '50s. I didn't let on that I had the money with me and for a moment or two I was uncertain about what I should do. But I remembered that whatever his virtues, trustworthiness certainly didn't seem to be one of them and I found it strange that he was in distress because studies were something that hardly ever took up his attention. I made some trite excuse or another and made off.

Once home, I told my father what had happened, smugly satisfied that I had not been duped. Father was silent for a while and then asked if it had occurred to me that Saroj's problem may have been genuine. How could I know it wasn't? It wasn't a bad idea to lend a man a hand when he was down—that, he said, should be the first instinct and not suspicion. Suppose the boy was telling the truth, how would I then face myself? Sure, one was bound to be let down sometimes, but as a rule trust was not betrayed. Even at that age I could see this as merely stubborn idealism, and a refusal to see that deception was always round the corner, but I chose not to argue.

My father suggested I carry the money to Saroj the next morning and that was what I did. He wasn't difficult to find and when I handed over the money he was at a loss for words, thanking me again and again for being there for him in his time of need. I came away with the afterglow of relief about the whole thing and my father was relieved that Saroj could now sit for his exams. I lost touch with him soon after, since I was preparing for my own exams, my routine narrowing down to school, studies at home and then back again to school the next morning, with very little time for anything else. My year-end exams were over and school closed for the long winter holidays. This was a lazy time, no pressure of any kind and I spent my days reading, walking the countryside, chatting with the Jesuits in school, sitting alone in the library, reading and occasionally taking trips to town.

On one such trip I was talking to the store owner who knew Saroj. I told him I hadn't seen him since the time my father had helped him with his school fees. Surprised, the man told me that it had been weeks since Saroj had quit school; the school authorities described him as a shirker with no affinity for studies. Angered, Saroj's father had taken him out of school, something the school evidently welcomed. Where was Saroj now? He had fallen out with his father in a quarrel, had got into bad company and absconded. Rumour was that he was in Ranchi to find fresher pastures.

It was depressing to know the truth. More than indignation at being duped, I was saddened that Saroj had proved himself to be a scapegrace after all. I felt no satisfaction that I'd been vindicated in my cynicism, but in spite of myself, I couldn't help a smile imagining my father's reaction. But I didn't have the heart to tell him when I got home.

Cronin's Race

Of the many Jesuit priests who taught us at St Xavier's, few were as firm in their views as Father Cronin; he was, so far as my memory goes, Father Prefect. He was a marvellous teacher. I still remember how we listened absorbed as he took us through Shakespeare's *Henry V*. But his world was one of simple demarcation between what was right and what wasn't. Basically, he handled situations from this standpoint, no ambiguity there at all. This was a simplistic way of looking at things, we used to tell ourselves.

It showed up in his approach to little humdrum things. If you deliberately ignored your responsibility, you were letting yourself down. If you were unfair to someone on purpose, you were letting yourself down. If you took advantage of the umpire's wrong decision in a cricket match, you were letting yourself down. Infraction on trivial matters could be simple error, nothing serious. On more serious matters they touched on the graver questions of right and wrong. Sometimes this could be trying. Although Fr Cronin's disposition was serious, it was by no means forbidding and we never failed to admire his complete sincerity. So what if he was a little strait-laced sometimes? He meant well and was there for us always when we had problems, helping us with our homework and games, and more importantly counselling on misunderstandings between boys.

A boy from a junior class often went to Fr Cronin for his athletics coaching. His name escapes me now, so I shall call him Lokesh. He was a natural sprinter in the 100 yards (as it was called then) and Fr Cronin coached him as often as he asked, after classes. I remember the days when Lokesh was put through his paces, Fr Cronin keeping time and helping him run faster. We knew Lokesh was sure to win the 75- and 100-yard dashes as he was clearly ahead of others. Fr Cronin, proud of his apprentice, did not spare Lokesh or himself in the training. Lokesh had a problem though. He had trouble with his start when the starter's gun sounded. He would invariably set off before the signal, and be called back to line before the race could begin again. This happened time after time. It annoyed everyone, Fr Cronin most of all. Repeatedly he urged Lokesh to control himself. Why couldn't he use a little discipline? But nothing seemed to work.

The main school event was two weeks away. This was the annual sports meet towards the end of the year. It was showcase stuff. Teams marching in their house colours—red for Britto, blue for Gonzaga, yellow for Loyola and green for Xavier—in bright winter sunshine. Throngs of spectators, including proud parents. The cups shining and on display. And Brother Slack, the MC, announcing the start of the sports in his impeccably elegant tone: 'Good afternoon, ladies and gentlemen. Welcome to our annual sports meeting.' The events then began: sprinting, long jump, high jump, and others. The chief attraction for many were the sprint events. First came the heats and then, for those qualifying, the finals.

Fr Cronin had coached Lokesh well and it was almost a given that Lokesh would win easily, but his starting problem refused to go away. At the heats, he went across the line before the start signal. The second try was his last, and the same mistake would disqualify him from the finals. Fr Cronin came up to him. Stay relaxed, and the race would be his, he told Lokesh. They lined up again and this time he broke no rules, qualifying effortlessly. I think among all of us Fr Cronin was the most relieved.

It was time for the final of the 100-yards dash. The runners lined up. Fr Cronin told Lokesh he was doing fine, but that he should remember this was the finals and he mustn't do anything silly and spoil it for himself. The starter's gun sounded and frustratingly, Lokesh started off before it did. Fr Cronin told Lokesh with all the restraint he could muster that he must remain calm. If others could, why couldn't he? It was time now for the second and final signal. The gun went off and the runners sprinted across the line. I don't recall what happened exactly, but we heard Fr Cronin call out, 'Out of the line, Lokesh. You're disqualified.'

This was a shock. None of us could tell if Lokesh had started before the signal. Had he or hadn't he? Obviously, Fr Cronin thought he had, which was why he disqualified him. Lokesh was shattered, feeling wronged and sorry for himself. Fr Cronin was grim in his disappointment as though it were his own failure.

The next day some of us gathered up the courage to ask him. Was he absolutely certain Lokesh had broken the rule? Yes he had, Father Cronin said. The point lay elsewhere, he said. It was only a school race. But was he to go through life as an adult without consideration for others, with neither the awareness nor the discipline to realize that over and over again, he was taking advantage? In the world of men where fundamental values were crucial, what would this make him? The point wasn't whether he broke the rule in a school event. It was to do with the fact that after so many warnings, he had allowed doubt to enter. A business as simple as this had no room for doubt. The fact that he had failed the fundamental requirements of simple discipline, responsibility, and respect for his peers was bad enough. Surely this was an exaggeration? Like skipping a traffic light, surely it was a simple error? Was it really? Fr Cronin asked. And please would we step down from our sanctimonious high ground? What he was saying was that fundamental integrity was not negotiable.

Innocuous as the incident was, I wondered whether Fr Cronin was justified in giving so much weightage to this affair. But one thing I knew for sure, right or wrong, logical or illogical, what he did was absolutely in character.

Know All

I don't remember his name. As a matter of fact, I don't think any of us knew it when he first showed up at school; but for a very good reason we simply called him Know All.

He didn't belong to St Xavier's, our school in Hazaribagh. He was visiting from Calcutta and staying with a relative. He looked amiable enough and was eighteen years old or so at the time. He was well-mannered and well-spoken, so when he greeted one of our Jesuit Fathers pleasantly one day, he immediately made an impression and was invited to visit our school. I've often thought back on it with mixed feelings. Was it a happy experience? Or was it not? Neither really, but the time with him was certainly quite beyond run-off-the-mill, and I can still laugh about it after so many years.

I was in my senior year in school which meant our visitor was older than us, and it was one of the reasons why we looked up to him. It was cricket season at school and matches between the four houses—Xavier, Britto, Loyola and Gonzaga—were the centre of excitement and the subject of all sorts of talk about how the games went, who did what, how the games could have turned out and what was likely to happen in the next match. Into this atmosphere walked Know All. He invariably came to watch the matches and we could see straightaway that he was something of an expert. In a very short time, we were reeling under the weight of his expertise.

Our main playground, though rather grandly named Balmoral, was very pretty in its own right. Lovely green surface, and fringed by a screen of eucalyptus which threw long shadows on the field as the day progressed. On crisp, cold Sunday mornings, the sun bright on the grass, it was all very scenic and watching the game was perhaps as enjoyable as being on the field.

Know All's presence cut across the ambience because he chattered non-stop during the matches, offering the benefit of his opinions. No, no, the field placing was all wrong. He would never set a field like that. Such and such fielder should move out deeper. There should be an extra man in the slips, and so on. The bowler was not bowling to his field. Another day it was the batsman who came under the scanner. Irritably, he said his footwork was all wrong and tentative.

Know All left us breathless and when we spoke about him to our mentors—Australian Jesuits who knew their cricket—they smiled in polite acknowledgement. Did Know All play cricket in Calcutta? Of course he did. He was a regular in his club team (which one this was he didn't say). What was his specialty? Modestly, he told us he was an all-rounder, bowling leg-breaks and coming in at number three in the batting order. He kept us captivated with his exploits: how one time he trapped an aggressive batsman into mistiming a hit and losing his wicket, how he took the wind out of the sails of a troublesome bowler, how everyone marvelled at his rate of scoring.

We wanted badly to see him in action and so we set up a friendly match on the Police Training Grounds beside our school where we often played. Know All at first vigorously rejected the idea, but gave in when we insisted. Know All's team took first strike. Know All came in after the fall of the first wicket. He was sheer presence at the crease as he adjusted his gloves, looked around at the field placings and crouched into his stance. He left the first ball alone, watching it go past the stumps. He did likewise on the second delivery and we knew here was a batsman who knew how to read a bowler and settle in. A ball or two later he made a sudden lunge and his off-stump went cartwheeling. It was so unexpected that we couldn't react. Know All came back, saying something about being unsighted.

It was now the turn of Know All's team to field. The ball was given to him sometime later. I remember that in one over, the batsman hit him for two fours and a six or something like that. At the end of the over, the captain gave him a searching look. It was all strategy, Know All said. In the next over, he was going to draw the batsman out of the crease for an easy stumping. And he was true to his word. We watched as he brought the batsman well beyond the crease, and we also watched as the batsman connected solidly to send the ball speeding across the line three times in the over. Know All trotted back to his fielding position and his captain didn't ask him to bowl again.

We felt terribly let down, completely at a loss.

Suddenly, in the beautiful winter afternoon, all our expectations having proved futile, cricket seemed charmless. Was Know All a huge fraud after all? Or was what we saw an aberration? We were resentful of this embarrassing anti-climax. When we shared this with our Jesuit priests, they replied tongue-in-cheek, with no attempt to disguise their humour. Father Moore said that Know All had perhaps downplayed himself, and had tried to save the opposite side from the blushes. Father Thwaites told us to cheer up and not feel let down. After all, it wasn't every day that we had the privilege of encountering such a stupendous authority of the game. It was another matter that Know All's knowledge belied his performance on the ground. It was also another matter he said, that the two rarely went hand-in-hand.

Grogs' Lessons

'How do you know Queen Cleopatra was beautiful? Where's the evidence?' The mark of a civilized mind was the readiness to re-examine accepted history. So Father Kevin Grogan, mentor of our youth, told us often.

Our rector, Father John Moore—'The Boss'—was a paternal figure. He was firm, fair, patient, and always concerned about the boys he was responsible for. We respected him deeply but we were wary of him because he was a plain-speaking, no-nonsense administrator who was committed to our well-being and at the same time firm with the parents when he needed to be. Father Grogan on the other hand could not have been more dissimilar. He was anything but a conscious mentor and his influence on our thinking and on ways we looked at things was far from deliberate. If anyone were to define him as moulder of young minds, he would have been horrified. But Fr Moore and Fr Grogan were close friends, they complemented each other and worked tirelessly for the growth of the school.

Most Jesuits we interacted with when we were small shared our world of boyhood—of schoolboy adventures, of cricket and football, of Billy Bunter and William, cowboys and Indians. At that age these were pure joy. Father Grogan took our classes three years or so before our school leaving Senior Cambridge exams. We quickly found out that 'Grogs' belonged more in the grown-ups' world, and it showed. It showed in the way he never disciplined us, though there were a great many things we could have been disciplined for. It was as though he felt that chastisement was something that was embarrassing to both the giver and the taker. He seldom showed real anger, but let us know he was disappointed if we said or did anything 'unworthy of a gentleman'.

Kevin Grogan was born in 1913 in a rural town in Australia's Northern Victoria, and he joined the Jesuits in 1931. He came to India in 1951 and, after working in villages in Chhotanagpur, came to St Xavier's in Hazaribagh. He loved talking to people, but his broken Hindi was a barrier. St Xavier's was an ideal platform for his flow of expression and ideas; soon we were won over by his gift as both raconteur and thoughtful communicator.

The Australian Fathers in Hazaribagh were unencumbered by dogma, a trait that was markedly pronounced in Grogs. He never preached, and he considered the very notion of dicta as ridiculous. He spoke and mixed with us with an easy informality, his kind blue eyes and friendly face alive with humour. We didn't see his classes as 'classes' in the usual sense. He had a special gift for words, enjoyed crosswords and composing limericks and opened up to us the elegance and beauty of English prose and lyrics. Teaching English, history and scripture, he took us through the texts and then beyond them and presented them in the perspectives of their time and their world. And he did this in his casual, conversational way. In his Bible classes he talked at length on the lives of Jews and early Christians in Judaea, the tyranny of Roman occupation, the political turmoil and the fear the Consul created in the people. Teaching us Sheridan's *The Rivals*, he brought us close to the temper of fashionable London society of the time, and regaled us with its quirks, its amorous intrigues, its genteel women and foppish men. Another time he introduced us to the mystery of the man who was Shakespeare and the question of who really wrote the plays. How far this freedom from the confines of texts served us in our examinations is moot, but many of us loved every bit of it.

My own best moments with Grogs were during the long summer and winter holidays. The school was quiet then and I frequently spent my time in the library or spent hours with Grogs. Those were lazy days. We talked ramblingly, and in our wandering conversations he returned, one way or another, to the matter of myths that history often perpetuated. Typically there was no earnestness to him, nothing showy, only a wry bemusement that many of these myths continued to hold currency. Quite suddenly, he came up with examples at random. Here are some I remember. One was about the accepted Christian story that Emperor Nero started Rome's great fire, and played the fiddle when the city was burning. He said Nero wasn't in Rome at all at the time of the fire. The other was about Lincoln's emancipation proclamation freeing the slaves; Grogs said that this was actually wartime strategy to preserve the Union, Lincoln had no real issues with slavery. Yet another one was about the unspeakable brutality of Governor John Eyre on the men, women and children of Jamaica at the time of the Morant Bay rebellion in the West Indies in 1865 when there was public outrage in Britain. Some of the staunchest supporters of Eyre's brutality were Charles Dickens and Thomas Carlyle—men revered in England for their righteousness and empathy for the oppressed. 'Great Authors, but so much for their humanism,' said Grogs. When talking about the French Revolution and the guillotine—we were discussing Conrad's *The Rover* which was set in that period—Grogs recalled that although that machine of execution was named after Joseph-Ignace Guillotin, he was not its inventor. The credit, he said, went to Antoine Louis, a surgeon and the actual inventor who designed the prototype. For some time after it was invented the contraption was called 'Louisette', he told us. Now and then Grogs came up with curiously interesting facts. For example, he once asked me if I knew that Suleiman the Magnificent, Sultan of the mighty Ottoman Empire was also an accomplished goldsmith.

When I spent time with Grogs during the holidays he never asked me how my studies were going, whether I was brushing up on my algebra and geometry which were my nemesis. He gave me books to read instead: 'Here, read this and tell me if you like it.' The essays of Lamb, Chesterton and Belloc, plays of Oscar Wilde and letters of Nehru, and various novels, Bronte's *Wuthering Heights,* Melville's *Moby Dick,* Graves' *I, Claudius* and Remarque's *All Quiet on the Western Front* were some of them. In the afternoon silence, he read out to me poems of Keats, Coleridge, Hopkins and Swinburne for the 'imagery and the music'. And he encouraged us to respect good prose.

Kevin Grogan was a chaplain with the Australian army during the Second World War on the island of Timor, now part of Indonesia, scene of some of the bloodiest fighting of the war. Its horrors had not twisted his sense of balance, something that was apparent in his humour. It was subtle, bordering sometimes on the risqué, and was sure to shock strait-laced sensibilities. Once a classmate badgered him for a very short story. Grogs thought for a second or two and gave us one. 'Three athletic girls went for a tramp in the woods,' he said. Pause. What then? 'The tramp died, didn't he, lads?' Someone asked Grogs for another witticism and he gave it to us. A voluptuous young woman went to a psychiatrist. As she lay on the couch, she said she found herself worrying sick over little things. 'Am I exaggerating, doctor?' She asked anxiously. The psychiatrist regarded her Junoesque figure and said gravely, 'Young lady, I believe you do have a talent for exaggerating beyond proportion.' Another day, Grogs reminded us that the early bird catches the worm. But what's in it for the worm? A bright spark asked. Grogs looked at him patiently and said, 'Lad, the worm was coming home.'

Even Grogs' reprimands carried a sly elegance. Once he set us a précis-writing assignment. My friend Aditi Nath, an illustrious student, allowed a not-so-bright classmate to copy his work, feeling sorry that he was clueless. Grogs returned our work the next day, calling out our names and ratings: very good, good, average and poor. While marking the papers he had known at once that Aditi Nath had willingly let his work be copied. First he announced the copier's rating: 'Very good,' he called out. He then announced Aditi Nath's rating: 'Very good rubbish,' he said in delightful paradox. The message was clear. Such inelegant collusion wouldn't wash with him. By reversing the ratings he was getting across his oblique reproof for both of them.

There were other sides to Grogs. Father Bill Dwyer, who was later the school's principal, told us that Grogs was an expert horseman, and also that when a film was being made on the life of Constant Lievens, the Belgian missionary, Grogs did the horse-riding scenes since the actor couldn't ride. He also taught us how to make stylish belts of interconnecting leather or plaited cord.

Father Grogan died on 30 November 1980. He was sixty-seven then. Till the day he died, Grogs kept alive his interest in the boys who had graduated, keeping track of where they were, and what they were doing. When I went to Hazaribagh in 1973, Grogs was delighted. My wife and I were fêted and pampered by the Fathers, some of whom I had studied under. Grogs asked me to address the senior class. He wanted me to share my thoughts on the 'wider world' of which, he hoped, St Xavier's was a microcosm. That was the last time I went to Hazaribagh and the last time I saw Father Grogan.

We often talked about our days with Grogs and the way many of us looked forward to his company beyond the classroom. He never had charge of a dormitory, but in the evenings many of us went to his room with our essays or simply for a chat because we were drawn to him for his concern, wit and warmth. He also had a special affinity for the less fortunate and his compassion for them was touching. As Father Dwyer recalled, for years Grogs was an active member of the Hazaribagh Lions Club, giving inspiration and ideas on how to help the poor. When famine broke out in 1966–67, he was the main organizer of the 'sasta roti' outlets which the Lions Club sponsored.

What was his bequest in measurable terms? Was it durable? Did it drive us to do well in examinations? Did he help prepare us for successful careers? What we remembered most were his presence and his observations—unpretentious and humorous—which gave us the insight into the kind of man he was, and his hopes for us. He talked to us about different values: decency, knowing right from wrong, saying no to the eroding power of envy, the importance of embracing curiosity that in his words was 'oxygen for the soul', the ability to laugh at oneself, and the instinct to take life not so seriously all the time. And he would say something else: Don't be unduly impressed by yourself, leave it for the others. These—he said often with no hint of pedantry whatsoever, and with a matter-of-factness—would define the persons we would grow into. Yes. Yes, Father.